Kubernetes on AWS

Deploy and manage production-ready Kubernetes clusters on AWS

Ed Robinson

BIRMINGHAM - MUMBAI

Kubernetes on AWS

Commissioning Editor: Gebin George
Acquisition Editor: Rahul Nair
Content Development Editor: Abhishek Jadhav
Technical Editor: Aditya Khadye
Copy Editor: Safis Editing
Project Coordinator: Jagdish Prabhu
Proofreader: Safis Editing
Indexer: Pratik Shirodkar
Graphics: Tom Scaria
Production Coordinator: Aparna Bhagat

First published: November 2018

Production reference: 1291118

Published by Packt Publishing Ltd.
Livery Place
35 Livery Street
Birmingham
B3 2PB, UK.

ISBN 978-1-78839-007-1

www.packtpub.com

Adrian, your support made this book possible

`mapt.io`

Mapt is an online digital library that gives you full access to over 5,000 books and videos, as well as industry leading tools to help you plan your personal development and advance your career. For more information, please visit our website.

Why subscribe?

- Spend less time learning and more time coding with practical eBooks and Videos from over 4,000 industry professionals

- Improve your learning with Skill Plans built especially for you

- Get a free eBook or video every month

- Mapt is fully searchable

- Copy and paste, print, and bookmark content

Packt.com

Did you know that Packt offers eBook versions of every book published, with PDF and ePub files available? You can upgrade to the eBook version at `www.packt.com` and as a print book customer, you are entitled to a discount on the eBook copy. Get in touch with us at `customercare@packtpub.com` for more details.

At `www.packt.com`, you can also read a collection of free technical articles, sign up for a range of free newsletters, and receive exclusive discounts and offers on Packt books and eBooks.

Contributors

About the author

Ed Robinson works as a senior site reliability engineer at Cookpad's global headquarters in Bristol, UK. He has been working with Kubernetes for the last three years, deploying clusters on AWS to deliver resilient and reliable services for global audiences. He is a contributor to several open source projects and is a maintainer of Træfık, the modern HTTP reverse proxy designed for containers and microservices.

About the reviewer

Manuel Tiago Pereira is a software engineer with vast experience of automating infrastructure provisioning and configuration for systems from development environments to highly available platforms for web applications. For the last couple of years, he has been invested in providing solid platforms for application deployments using Kubernetes. He has dedicated most of his professional career to SaaS companies and he's currently working at Talkdesk in order to make life easier for call-center operators and increase their customers' happiness.

Packt is searching for authors like you

If you're interested in becoming an author for Packt, please visit authors.packtpub.com and apply today. We have worked with thousands of developers and tech professionals, just like you, to help them share their insight with the global tech community. You can make a general application, apply for a specific hot topic that we are recruiting an author for, or submit your own idea.

Table of Contents

Preface

Docker containers promise to radically change the way developers and operations build, deploy, and manage applications running on the cloud. Kubernetes provides the orchestration tools you need to realize that promise in production.

Kubernetes on AWS guides you in deploying a production-ready Kubernetes cluster on the **Amazon Web Services (AWS)** platform. You will discover how to use the power of Kubernetes, which is one of the fastest growing platforms for production-based container orchestration, to manage and update your applications. Kubernetes is becoming the go-to choice for production-grade deployments of cloud-native applications. This book covers Kubernetes from first principles. You will start by learning about Kubernetes' powerful abstractions—pods and services—which make managing container deployments easy. This will be followed by a guided tour through setting up a production-ready Kubernetes cluster on AWS, while learning the techniques you need to successfully deploy and manage your own applications.

By the end of the book, you will have gained plenty of hands-on experience with Kubernetes on AWS. You will also have picked up some tips on deploying and managing applications, keeping your cluster and applications secure, and ensuring that your whole system is reliable and resilient to failure.

Who this book is for

If you're a cloud engineer, cloud solution provider, sysadmin, site reliability engineer, or developer with an interest in DevOps and are looking for an extensive guide to running Kubernetes in the AWS environment, this book is for you. Though any previous knowledge of Kubernetes is not expected, some experience with Linux and Docker containers would be a bonus.

What this book covers

Chapter 1, *Google's Infrastructure for the Rest of Us*, helps you understand how Kubernetes can give you some of the same superpowers that the site reliability engineers at Google use to ensure that Google's services are resilient, reliable, and efficient.

Chapter 2, *Start Your Engines*, helps you take your first steps with Kubernetes. You will learn how to start a cluster suitable for learning and development use on your own workstation, and will begin to learn how to use Kubernetes itself.

Chapter 3, *Reach for the Cloud*, teaches you how to build a Kubernetes cluster running on AWS from first principles.

Chapter 4, *Managing Change in Your Applications*, gets into depth with tools that Kubernetes provide to manage the Pods that you run on your cluster.

Chapter 5, *Managing Complex Applications with Helm*, teaches you about how you can deploy a service to your cluster using a community-maintained chart.

Chapter 6, *Planning for Production*, gives you an idea of the myriad different options and decisions you can make when deciding to run Kubernetes in a production environment.

Chapter 7, *A Production-Ready Cluster*, helps you build a fully functional cluster that will serve as a base configuration to build upon for many different use cases.

Chapter 8, *Sorry My App Ate the Cluster*, delves into configuring pods with a different quality of service so important workloads are guaranteed the resources they need, but less important workloads can make use of idle resources when they are available without needing dedicated resources.

Chapter 9, *Storing State*, is all about using the deep integration that Kubernetes has with the AWS native storage solution Elastic Block Store (EBS).

Chapter 10, *Managing Container Images*, helps you understand how to leverage the AWS Elastic Container Registry (ECR) service to store your container images in a manner that tackles all these needs.

Chapter 11, *Monitoring and Logging*, teaches you how to set up a log management pipeline, and will help you understand some of the pitfalls and potential issues with logs. By the end of the chapter, you will have set up a metrics and alerting system. For this chapter refer to https://www.packtpub.com/sites/default/files/downloads/Monitoring_and_Logging.pdf.

Chapter 12, *Best Practices of Security*, teaches you how to manage a secure network for your Kubernetes cluster using both AWS and Kubernetes networking primitives. You will also learn how to keep your host operating systems secured. For this chapter refer to https://www.packtpub.com/sites/default/files/downloads/Best_Practices_of_Security.pdf.

To get the most out of this book

You will need access to an AWS account for performing the examples given in this book.

Download the example code files

You can download the example code files for this book from your account at www.packt.com. If you purchased this book elsewhere, you can visit www.packt.com/support and register to have the files emailed directly to you.

You can download the code files by following these steps:

1. Log in or register at www.packt.com.
2. Select the **SUPPORT** tab.
3. Click on **Code Downloads & Errata**.
4. Enter the name of the book in the **Search** box and follow the onscreen instructions.

Once the file is downloaded, please make sure that you unzip or extract the folder using the latest version of:

- WinRAR/7-Zip for Windows
- Zipeg/iZip/UnRarX for Mac
- 7-Zip/PeaZip for Linux

The code bundle for the book is also hosted on GitHub at https://github.com/PacktPublishing/Kubernetes-on-AWS. In case there's an update to the code, it will be updated on the existing GitHub repository.

We also have other code bundles from our rich catalog of books and videos available at https://github.com/PacktPublishing/. Check them out!

Conventions used

There are a number of text conventions used throughout this book.

`CodeInText`: Indicates code words in text, database table names, folder names, filenames, file extensions, pathnames, dummy URLs, user input, and Twitter handles. Here is an example: "Mount the downloaded `WebStorm-10*.dmg` disk image file as another disk in your system."

A block of code is set as follows:

```
html, body, #map {
  height: 100%;
  margin: 0;
  padding: 0
}
```

When we wish to draw your attention to a particular part of a code block, the relevant lines or items are set in bold:

```
[default]
exten => s,1,Dial(Zap/1|30)
exten => s,2,Voicemail(u100)
exten => s,102,Voicemail(b100)
exten => i,1,Voicemail(s0)
```

Any command-line input or output is written as follows:

```
$ mkdir css
$ cd css
```

Bold: Indicates a new term, an important word, or words that you see onscreen. For example, words in menus or dialog boxes appear in the text like this. Here is an example: "Select **System info** from the **Administration** panel."

Warnings or important notes appear like this.

Tips and tricks appear like this.

Get in touch

Feedback from our readers is always welcome.

General feedback: If you have questions about any aspect of this book, mention the book title in the subject of your message and email us at customercare@packtpub.com.

Errata: Although we have taken every care to ensure the accuracy of our content, mistakes do happen. If you have found a mistake in this book, we would be grateful if you would report this to us. Please visit www.packt.com/submit-errata, selecting your book, clicking on the Errata Submission Form link, and entering the details.

Piracy: If you come across any illegal copies of our works in any form on the Internet, we would be grateful if you would provide us with the location address or website name. Please contact us at copyright@packt.com with a link to the material.

If you are interested in becoming an author: If there is a topic that you have expertise in and you are interested in either writing or contributing to a book, please visit authors.packtpub.com.

Reviews

Please leave a review. Once you have read and used this book, why not leave a review on the site that you purchased it from? Potential readers can then see and use your unbiased opinion to make purchase decisions, we at Packt can understand what you think about our products, and our authors can see your feedback on their book. Thank you!

For more information about Packt, please visit packt.com.

1
Google's Infrastructure for the Rest of Us

Kubernetes was originally built by some of the engineers at Google who were responsible for their internal container scheduler, Borg.

Learning how to run your own infrastructure with Kubernetes can give you some of the same superpowers that the site reliability engineers at Google utilize to ensure that Google's services are resilient, reliable, and efficient. Using Kubernetes allows you to make use of the knowledge and expertise that engineers at Google and other companies have built up by virtue of their massive scale.

Your organization may never need to operate at the scale of a company such as Google. You will, however, discover that many of the tools and techniques developed in companies that operate on clusters of tens of thousands of machines are applicable to organizations running much smaller deployments.

While it is clearly possible for a small team to manually configure and operate tens of machines, the automation needed at larger scales can make your life simpler and your software more reliable. And if you later need to scale up from tens of machines to hundreds or even thousands, you'll know that the tools you are using have already been battle tested in the harshest of environments.

The fact that Kubernetes even exists at all is both a measure of the success and a vindication of the open source/free software movement. Kubernetes began as a project to open source an implementation of the ideas and research behind Google's internal container orchestration system, Borg. Now it has taken on a life of its own, with the majority of its code now being contributed by engineers outside of Google.

The story of Kubernetes is not only one of Google seeing the benefits that open sourcing its own knowledge would indirectly bring to its own cloud business, but it's also one of the open source implementations of the various underlying tools that were needed coming of age.

Linux containers had existed in some form or another for almost a decade, but it took the Docker project (first open sourced in 2013) for them to become widely used and understood by a large enough number of users. While Docker did not itself bring any single new underlying technology to the table, its innovation was in packaging the tools that already existed in a simple and easy-to-use interface.

Kubernetes was also made possible by the existence of etcd, a key-value store based on the Raft consensus algorithm that was also first released in 2013 to form the underpinnings of another cluster scheduling tool that was being built by CoreOS. For Borg, Google had used an underlying state store based on the very similar Paxos algorithm, making etcd the perfect fit for Kubernetes.

Google were prepared to take the initiative to create an open source implementation of the knowledge which, up until that point, had been a big competitive advantage for their engineering organization at a time when Linux containers were beginning to become more popular thanks to the influence of Docker.

Kubernetes, Docker, etcd, and many other tools that form the Linux container ecosystem are written with the Go programming language. Go provides all the features that are needed to build systems such as these, with excellent first-class support for concurrency and great networking libraries built in.

However, in my view, the simplicity of the language itself makes it such a good choice for open source infrastructure tools, because such a wide variety of developers can pick up the basics of the language in a few hours and start making productive contributions to a project.

If you are interested in finding out more about the go programming language, you could try taking a look at `https://tour.golang.org/welcome/1` and then spend an hour looking at `https://gobyexample.com`.

Why do I need a Kubernetes cluster?

At its core, Kubernetes is a container scheduler, but it is a much richer and fully featured toolkit that has many other features. It is possible to extend and augment the functionality that Kubernetes provides, as products such as RedHat's OpenShift have done. Kubernetes also allows you to extend it's core functionality yourself by deploying add-on tools and services to your cluster.

Here are some of the key features that are built into Kubernetes:

- **Self-healing**: Kubernetes controller-based orchestration ensures that containers are restarted when they fail, and rescheduled when the nodes they are running on fail. User-defined health checks allow users to make decisions about how and when to recover from failing services, and how to direct traffic when they do.
- **Service discovery**: Kubernetes is designed from the ground up to make service discovery simple without needing to make modifications to your applications. Each instance of your application gets its own IP address, and standard discovery mechanisms such as DNS and load balancing let your services communicate.
- **Scaling**: Kubernetes makes horizontal scaling possible at the push of a button, and also provides autoscaling facilities.
- **Deployment orchestration**: Kubernetes not only helps you to manage running applications, but has tools to roll out changes to your application and its configuration. Its flexibility allows you to build complex deployment patterns for yourself or to use one of a number of add-on tools.
- **Storage management**: Kubernetes has built-in support for managing the underlying storage technology on cloud providers, such as AWS Elastic Block Store volumes, as well as other standard networked storage tools, such as NFS.
- **Cluster optimization**: The Kubernetes scheduler automatically assigns your workloads to machines based on their requirements, allowing for better utilization of resources.
- **Batch workloads**: As well as long-running workloads, Kubernetes can also manage batch jobs, such as CI, batch processing, and cron jobs.

The roots of containers

Ask the average user what a Docker container is and you might get any one of a dozen responses. You might be told something about lightweight virtual machines, or how it is that this hot new disruptive technology is going to revolutionize computing. In reality, Linux containers are certainly not a new idea, nor are they really all that much like a virtual machine.

Back in 1979, the `chroot syscall` was added to Version 7 of Unix. Calling chroot changes the apparent root directory for the current running process and its subprocesses. Running a program in a so-called chroot jail prevents it from accessing files outside of the specified directory tree.

One of the first uses of chroot was for testing of the BSD build system, something that is inherited by the package build systems of most of our modern Linux distributions, such as Debian, RedHat, and SuSE. By testing packages in a clean chrooted environment, build scripts can detect missing dependency information.

Chroot is also commonly used to sandbox untrusted processes-for example, shell processes on shared FTP or SFTP servers. Systems designed specifically with security in mind, such as the Postfix mail transfer agent, utilize chroot to isolate individual components of a pipeline in order to prevent a security issue in one component from rippling across the system.

Chroot is in fact a very simple isolation tool that was never intended to provide either security or control over anything other than the filesystem access of the processes. For its intended purpose of providing filesystem isolation for the likes of build tools, it is perfect. But for isolating applications in a production environment, we need a little more control.

Enter the container

Trying to understand what a Linux container is can be a little difficult. As far as the Linux kernel is concerned, there is no such thing as a container. The kernel has a number of features that allow a process to be isolated, but these features are much lower-level and granular than what we now think of as a container. Container engines such as Docker use two main kernel features to isolate processes:

Cgroups

Cgroups, or control groups, provide an interface for controlling one or a group of processes, hence the name. They allow the control of several aspects of the group's use of resources. Resource utilization can be controlled using a limit (for example, by limiting memory usage). Cgroups also allow priorities to be set to give processes a greater or lesser share of time-bound resources, such as CPU utilization or I/O. Cgroups can also be used to snapshot (and restore) the state of running processes.

Namespaces

The other part of the container puzzle is kernel namespaces. They operate in a manner that is somewhat similar to our use of the chroot syscall in that a container engine instructs the kernel to only allow the process a particular view of the system's resources.

Instead of just limiting access to the filesystem kernel, namespaces limit access to a number of different resources.

Each process can be assigned to a namespace and can then only see the resources connected to that namespace. The kinds of resources that can be namespaced are as follows:

- **Mount**: Mount namespaces control access to the filesystem.
- **Users**: Each namespace has its own set of user IDs. User ID namespaces are nested, and thus a user in a higher-level namespace can be mapped to another in a lower level. This is what allows a container to run processes as root, without giving that process full permission to the root system.
- **PID**: The process ID namespace, like the users namespace, is nested. This is why the host can see the processes running inside of the containers when inspecting the process list on a system that is running containers. However, inside of the namespace the numbers are different; this means that the first process created inside a PID namespace, can be assigned PID 1, and can inherit zombie processes if required.
- **Network**: A network namespace contains one or more network interfaces. The namespace has its own private network resources, such as addresses, the routing table, and firewall.

 There are also namespaces for IPC, UTS, and for the Cgroups interface itself.

Putting the pieces together

It is the job of the container engine (software such as Docker or rkt) to put these pieces together and make something usable and understandable for us mere mortals.

While a system that directly exposed all of the details of Cgroups and namespaces would be very flexible, it would be far harder to understand and manage. Using a system such as Docker gives us a simple-to-understand abstraction over these low-level concepts, but necessarily makes many decisions for us about how these low-level concepts are used.

The fundamental breakthrough that Docker made over previous container technologies was to take great defaults for isolating a single process and combine them with an image format that allows developers to provide all the dependencies that the process requires to run correctly.

This is an incredibly good thing because it allows anyone to install Docker and quickly understand what is going on. It also makes this kind of Linux container the perfect building block to build larger and more complex systems, such as Kubernetes.

Here, schedule this...

At its heart, Kubernetes is a system for scheduling work to a cluster of computers—a scheduler. But why would you want a scheduler?

If you think about your own systems, then you'll realize that you probably already have a scheduler, but unless you are already using something like Kubernetes, it might look very different.

Perhaps your scheduler is a team of people, with spreadsheets and documentation about which services run on each server in your data center. Perhaps that team of people looks at past traffic statistics to try and guess when there will be a heavy load in the future. Perhaps your scheduler relies on your users alerting members of your team at any time of the night if your applications stop functioning.

This book is about these problems, about how we can move on from a world of manual processes and making guesses about the future usage of our systems. It is about harnessing the skill and experience of the humans that administer the systems to encode our operational knowledge into systems that can make decisions about your running system second by second, seamlessly responding to crashed processes, failed machines, and increased load without any human intervention.

Kubernetes chooses to model its scheduler as a control loop so that the system is constantly discovering the current state of the cluster, comparing it to a desired state, and then taking actions to reduce the difference between the desired and the actual state. This is summarized in the following diagram:

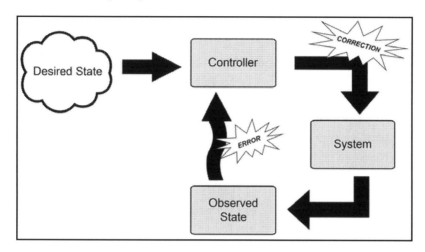

A typical control loop

Being able to declare the state that we want the system to be in, and then have the system itself take the actions needed to manifest that desired state, is very powerful.

You may previously have used an imperative tool or a script to manage a system, or you may even have used a written playbook of the manual steps to take. This sort of approach is very much like a recipe: you take a set of actions one after another and hopefully end up in the state that you desire.

This works well when describing how to install and bootstrap a system for the first time, but when you need to run your script against a system that is already running, your logic needs to become more complicated as, for each stage in your recipe, you have to stop and check what needs to be done before you do it.

When using a declarative tool such as Kubernetes to manage your system, your configuration is simplified and becomes much easier to reason about. One important side effect of this approach is that Kubernetes will repair your configuration if an underlying failure causes it to drift away from your desired state.

By combining control loops and declarative configuration, Kubernetes allows you to tell it what to do for you, not how to do it. Kubernetes gives you, the operator, the role of the architect and Kubernetes takes the role of the builder. An architect provides a builder with detailed plans for a building, but doesn't need to explain how to build the walls with bricks and mortar. Your responsibility is to provide Kubernetes with a specification of your application and the resources it needs, but you don't need to worry about the details of exactly how and where it will run.

The basics of Kubernetes

Let's begin our look at Kubernetes by looking at some of the fundamental concepts that most of Kubernetes is built upon. Getting a clear understanding of how these core building blocks fit together will serve you well as we explore the multitude of features and tools that comprise Kubernetes.

It can be a little confusing to use Kubernetes without a clear understanding of these core building blocks so, if you don't have any experience with Kubernetes, you should take your time to understand how these pieces fit together before moving on.

The pod

Like a group of whales, or perhaps a pea pod, a Kubernetes pod is a group of linked containers. As the following diagram shows, a pod can be made up of one or more containers; often a pod might just be a single container:

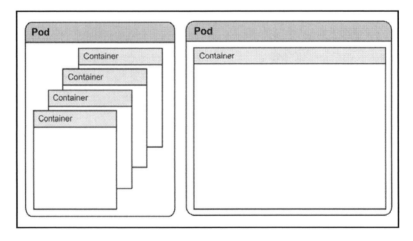

Pods are a logical grouping of one or more containers

Each pod that Kubernetes schedules is allocated its own unique IP address. The network namespace (and thus the pod's IP address) is shared by each container in the pod.

This means that it is convenient to deploy several containers together that closely collaborate over the network. For example, you might deploy a reverse proxy alongside a web application to add SSL or caching capabilities to an application that does not natively support them. In the following example, we achieve this by deploying a typical web application server-for example, Ruby on Rails—alongside a reverse proxy—for example, NGINX. This additional container provides further capabilities that might not be provided by the native application. This pattern of composing functionality together from smaller isolated containers means that you are able to reuse components more easily, and makes it simple to add additional functionality to existing tools. The setup is shown in the following diagram:

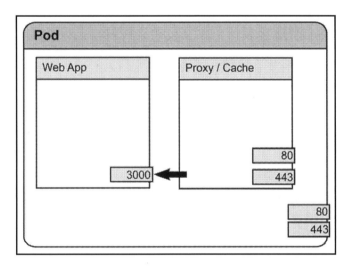

Providing additional capabilities by composing multiple containers

As well as sharing the network namespace, Kubernetes also allows very flexible sharing of volume mounts between any number of containers in a pod. This allows for a number of scenarios where several components may collaborate to perform a particular task.

In this example, we are using three containers that coordinate to serve a website built with a static-site generator using the NGINX webserver.

The first container uses Git to pull and update the source code from a remote Git repository. This repository is cloned into a volume that is shared with the second container. This second container uses the Jekyll framework to build the static files that will be served by our webserver. Jekyll watches the shared directory for changes on the filesystem and regenerates any files that need to be updated.

The directory that Jekyll writes the generated files to is shared with a container running NGINX that serves HTTP requests for our website, as shown in the following diagram:

 We are using Jekyll here as an example, but there are many tools you can use to build static websites, such as Hugo, Hexo, and Gatsby. Splitting your application into separate containers like this means that it is simple to upgrade a single component, or even try an alternative tool.

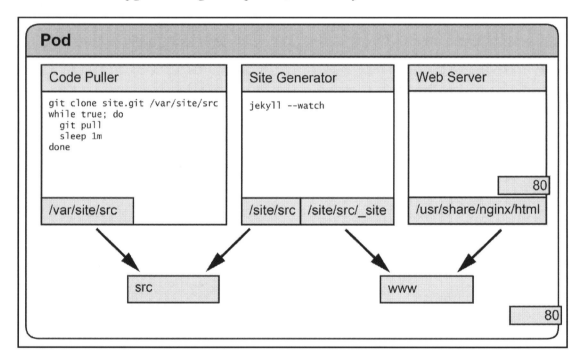

Another use for pods that share volume mounts is to support applications that communicate using Unix sockets, as shown in the following diagram. For example, an **extract transform load (ETL)** system could be modeled as several independent processes that communicate with UNIX sockets. This might be beneficial if you are able to make use of third-party tools for some or all of your pipeline, or reuse tools that you may have built for internal use in a variety of situations:

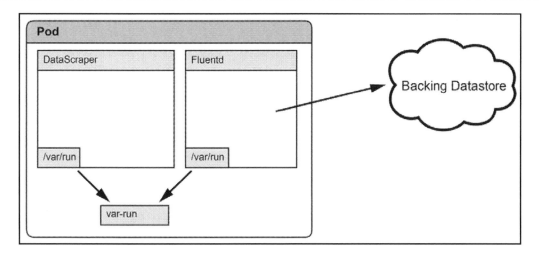

In this example, a custom application designed to scrape data from webpages communicates with an instance of Fluentd over a Unix domain socket located in a shared volume. The pattern of using a third-party tool such as Fluentd to push data to a backing datastore not only simplifies the implementation of the custom tool, but also provides compatibility with any store that Fluentd chooses to support.

Kubernetes gives you some strong guarantees that the containers in your pod have a shared lifecycle. This means that when you launch a pod, you can be sure that each container will be scheduled to the same node; this is important because it means that you can depend on the fact that other containers in your pod will exist and will be local. Pods are often a convenient way to glue the functionality of several different containers together, enabling the reuse of common components. You might, for example, use a sidecar container to enhance the networking abilities of your application, or provide additional log management or monitoring facilities.

Labeling all the things

Labels are key-value pairs that are attached to resources, such as pods. They are intended to contain information that helps you to identify a particular resource.

You might add labels to your pods to identify the application that is being run, as well as other metadata, such as a version number, an environment name, or other labels that pertain to your application.

Labels are very flexible, as Kubernetes leaves it up to you to label your own resources as you see fit.

Once you begin working with Kubernetes, you will discover that you are able to add labels to almost every resource that you create.

The power of being able to add labels that reflect the architecture of your own application is that you are able to use selectors to query the resources using any combination of the labels that you have given your resources. This setup is shown in the following diagram:

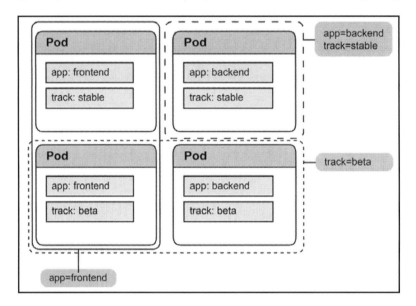

You can add labels to many of the resources that you will create in Kubernetes and then query them with selectors.

 Kubernetes doesn't enforce any particular schema or layout for the labels you give to objects in your cluster; and you are free to label your applications however you choose. If you want a little more structure however. Kubernetes does make some suggestions for labels you might want to apply to objects that can be grouped together into a logical Application. You can read more about this in the Kubernetes documentation: https://kubernetes.io/docs/concepts/overview/ working-with-objects/common-labels/.

Replica sets

In Kubernetes, a `ReplicaSet` is a resource that templates the creation of pods. The definition of a replica set contains a template definition of the pods that it creates, a desired count of replicas, and a selector to discover the pods under its management.

The `ReplicaSet` is used to ensure that the desired number of pods is always running. If the count of pods matching the selector drops below the desired count, then Kubernetes will schedule another.

Because the life of a pod is tied to that of the node that it is running on, a pod can be considered ephemeral. There are a number of reasons why the life of a particular pod could come to an end. Perhaps it was removed by the operator or an automated process. Kubernetes could have evicted the pod to better utilize the resources of the cluster or prepare the node for shutdown or restart. Or perhaps the underlying node failed.

A `ReplicaSet` allows us to manage our application by asking the cluster to ensure that the correct number of replicas is running across the cluster as a whole. This is a strategy that Kubernetes embraces across many of its APIs.

As a cluster operator, Kubernetes takes some of the complexity of running applications away from the user. When I decide that I need three instances of my application running, I no longer need to think about the underlying infrastructure: I can just tell Kubernetes to carry out my wishes. And if the worst happens and one of the underlying machines that my application is running on fails, Kubernetes will know how to self-heal my application and launch a new pod. No more pager calls and trying to recover or replace failed instances in the middle of the night.

> `ReplicaSet` replaces the `ReplicationController` that you might have read about in older tutorials and documentation. They are almost entirely identical, but differ in a few small ways.

Often, we want to update the software we run on our cluster. Because of this, we don't normally directly use `ReplicaSet` but, instead, manage them with a `Deployment` object. Deployments are used in Kubernetes to gracefully roll out new versions of a `ReplicaSet`. You will learn more about deployments in `Chapter 4`, *Managing Change in Your Applications*.

Services

The final basic tool that Kubernetes gives us to manage our applications is the service. **Services** give us a convenient way of accessing our services within our cluster, something often referred to as *service discovery*.

In practice, a service allows us to define a label selector to refer to a group of pods and then map that to something that our application can consume, without having to be modified to query the Kubernetes API to gather this information. Typically, a service will provide a stable IP address or DNS name that can be used to access the underlying pods that it refers to in a round robin fashion.

By using a service, our applications don't need to know that they are running on Kubernetes-we just need to configure them correctly with the DNS name or IP address of a service that they depend on.

A service provides a way for other applications in the cluster to discover pods that match a particular label selector. It does this by providing a stable IP address and, optionally, a DNS name. This setup is shown in the following diagram:

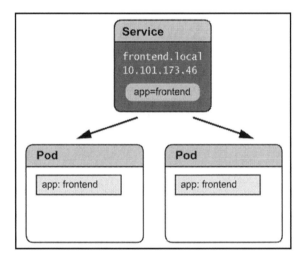

Under the hood

Now we have learned a little about the functionality that Kubernetes provides to us, the user, let's go a little deeper and look at the components that Kubernetes uses to implement these features. Kubernetes makes this task a little easier for us by having a microservice architecture, so we can look at the function of each component in a certain degree of isolation.

We will get our hands dirty over the next few chapters by actually deploying and configuring these components ourselves. However for now, let's start by getting a basic understanding of the function of each of these components by looking at the following diagram:

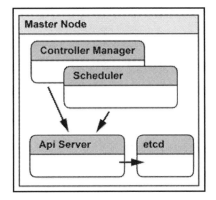

The main Kubernetes components on the master node

API server

The **API server** acts as Kubernetes' central hub. All the other components in Kubernetes communicate by reading, watching, and updating resources in Kubernetes APIs. This central component is used for all of the access and manipulation of information about the current state of the cluster, allowing Kubernetes to be extended and augmented with new features while still maintaining a high degree of consistency.

Kubernetes uses etcd to store the current state of the cluster. An etcd store is used because its design means that it is both resistant to failure and has strong guarantees of its consistency. However, the different components that make up Kubernetes never directly interact with etcd; instead, they communicate with the API server. This is a good design for us, the operator of a cluster, because it allows us to restrict access to etcd only to the API server component, improving security and simplifying management.

While the API server is the component in the Kubernetes architecture that everything else communicates with to access or update the state, it is stateless itself, with all storage being deferred to the backing etcd cluster. This again is an ideal design decision for us as cluster operators since it allows us to deploy multiple instances of the API server (if we wish) to provide high availability.

Controller manager

The **controller manager** is the service that runs the core control loops (or controllers) that implement some of core functionality that makes Kubernetes function. Each of these controllers watches the state of the cluster through the API server and then makes changes to try and move the state of the cluster closer to the desired state. The design of the controller manager means that only one instance of it should be running at a given time; however, to simplify deployment in a high-availability configuration, the controller manager has a built-in leader election functionality, so that several instances can be deployed side by side, but only one will actually carry out work at any one time.

Scheduler

The **scheduler** is perhaps the single most important component that makes Kubernetes a useful and practical tool. It watches for new pods in the unscheduled state, and then analyzes the current state of the cluster with regard to running workloads, available resources, and other policy-based issues. It then decides the best place for that pod to be run in. As with the controller manager, a single instance of the scheduler works at any one time, but in a high-availability configuration, leader election is available.

Kubelet

The **kubelet** is the agent that runs on each node, and is responsible for launching pods. It doesn't directly run containers but instead controls a runtime, such as Docker or rkt. Typically, the kubelet watches the API server to discover which pods have been scheduled on its node.

The kubelet operates at the level of `PodSpec`, so it only knows how to launch pods. Any of the higher-level concepts in the Kubernetes API are implemented by controllers that ultimately create or destroy pods with a specific configuration.

The kubelet also runs a tool called **cadvisior** that collects metrics about resource usage on the node, and using each container that is running on the node, this information can then be used by Kubernetes when making scheduling decisions.

Summary

By now, you should have a basic understanding of the stack of software that makes a modern container orchestrator like Kubernetes tick.

You should now understand the following:

- Containers are built on top of much lower-level features in the Linux kernel, such as namespaces and Cgroups.
- In Kubernetes a pod is a powerful abstraction that is built on top of containers.
- Kubernetes uses control loops to build a powerful system that allows the operator to declaratively specify what should be running. Kubernetes automatically takes actions to drive the system towards this state. This is the source of Kubernetes' self-healing properties.
- Nearly everything in Kubernetes can be given a label, and you should label your resources in order to make managing them simpler.

In the next chapter, you will gain some practical experience using the Kubernetes APIs by running a small cluster on your workstation.

Start Your Engines 2

In this chapter, we will be taking our first steps with Kubernetes. You will learn how to start a cluster suitable for learning and development use on your own workstation, and will begin to learn how to use Kubernetes itself. In this chapter, we will do the following:

- Learn how to install and use Minikube to run Kubernetes
- Build a simple application that runs in a Docker container
- Use Kubernetes to run simple applications

Your own Kubernetes

Minikube is a tool that makes it easy to run a simple Kubernetes cluster on your workstation. It is very useful, as it allows you to test your applications and configurations locally and quickly iterate on your applications without needing access to a larger cluster. For our purposes, it is the ideal tool to get some practical hands-on experience with Kubernetes. It is very simple to install and configure, as you will discover.

Installation

You will need a few tools to get Kubernetes running on your workstation:

- `kubectl` is the Kubernetes command-line interface. Throughout this book, you will be using it to interact with Kubernetes.

 In the Kubernetes community, no one agrees how to pronounce `kubectl`.

Try out these different ways and choose your favorite:

```
kube-kuttle
kube-control
kube-cee-tee-ell
kube-cuddle
```

- `minikube` is a command that manages Kubernetes on your local machine. It handles all the hard stuff, so you can get started with Kubernetes straight away.
- `docker`, the `minikube` virtual machine, has the Docker daemon running internally, but you might need the Docker command line installed on your workstation if you want to interact with it directly.

It is best to use Minikube in conjunction with a virtual machine, as platforms like macOS and Windows don't natively support Linux containers, and even on Linux it helps to keep your environment clean and isolated. There are various virtualization tools you can use with `minikube,` depending on your operating system:

- **VirtualBox**: It is simple to use and can be installed on macOS, Windows, and Linux.
- **VMware Fusion**: It is a commercial tool available on macOS.
- **KVM**: It is a well-known Linux virtualization tool.
- **xhyve**: It is an open source project that utilizes the native hypervisor framework in macOS. It performs very well but can be a little harder to install and use.
- **Hyper-V**: It is the native virtualization tool for Windows. Remember, you might need to manually enable it on your machine and set up its networking.

In this book, we are going to cover the default option, VirtualBox, but if you are using Minikube regularly, you might want to explore some of the other options, as they can be more performant and reliable if set up correctly.

You can find some documentation about the different drivers available at https://git.k8s.io/minikube/docs/drivers.md.

macOS

On a Mac, the best way to install `minikube` and `kubectl` is with the Homebrew package manager.

 The Homebrew package manager for macOS is a simple way to install development tools. You can find out how to install it on the website: `https://brew.sh/`.

1. Start by installing the Kubernetes command-line client `kubectl`:

   ```
   brew install kubernetes-cli
   ```

2. Next, install `minikube` and `virtualbox`:

   ```
   brew cask install minikube virtualbox
   ```

Linux

On Linux, the simplest installation method is to download and install pre-built binaries:

1. You should download the binaries for `minikube` and `kubectl`:

   ```
   curl -Lo minikube
   https://storage.googleapis.com/minikube/releases/latest/minikube-linux-amd64
   curl -LO https://dl.k8s.io/v1.10.6/bin/linux/amd64/kubectl
   ```

2. Once you have downloaded the binaries, make them executable and move them to somewhere on your path:

   ```
   chmod +x minikube kubectl
   sudo mv minikube kubectl /usr/local/bin/
   ```

The method of installing VirtualBox on Linux will depend on your distribution.

 Take a look at the instructions on the VirtualBox website: `https://www.virtualbox.org/wiki/Linux_Downloads`.

Windows

Installing Minikube on a Windows machine is as simple as it is on Linux or macOS.

Start by installing VirtualBox.

You can download the Windows installer for VirtualBox from `https://www.virtualbox.org/wiki/Downloads`.

If you are using the chocolatey package manager, perform the following steps:

1. Install `minikube`:

```
C:\> choco install minikube
```

2. Install `kubectl`:

```
C:\> choco install kubernetes-cli
```

   If you are not using chocolatey, you can manually install `minikube` and `kubectl`.

3. Download `minikube` at
   `https://storage.googleapis.com/minikube/releases/latest/minikube-windows-amd64.exe` and rename it to `minikube.exe`. Then move it to a location on your path. Download `kubectl`:
   `https://dl.k8s.io/v1.10.6/bin/windows/amd64/kubectl.exe` and then move it to a location on your path.

Starting Minikube

Once you have got `minikube` and your chosen virtualization tool installed, we can use it to build and start a local Kubernetes cluster.

If you choose to use `minikube` tool's default settings, doing so couldn't be simpler. Just run:

```
minikube start
```

You should then see some output, similar to the following:

```
Starting local Kubernetes v1.10.0 cluster...
Starting VM...
Getting VM IP address...
Moving files into cluster...
Setting up certs...
Connecting to cluster...
```

```
Setting up kubeconfig...
Starting cluster components...
Kubectl is now configured to use the cluster.
```

`minikube` start has many options that can be used to configure the cluster that is launched. Try running `minikube` help start to find out what you can customize.

You might want to set `--cpus` and/or `--memory` to customize how much of your computer's resources are used for the Minikube VM.

Assuming that everything went as expected, that's it; you should have a cluster installed and running on your local machine.

 The kubectl `config` file (found at `~/.kube/config` by default) defines contexts. A context links to a cluster and a user object. The cluster defines how.

The `minikube start` command creates a `kubectl` context pointing to the API server running within the Minikube VM, and is correctly configured with a user that will allow access to Kubernetes.

As you progress through this book, you will of course want to add additional contexts in order to connect to remote clusters that you many have set up. You should be able to switch back to the `minikube` context whenever you want to use `minikube` by running the following command:

```
kubectl config use-context minikube
```

First steps with kubectl

Let's start by validating that `kubectl` has indeed been configured to use your cluster correctly and that we can connect to it:

```
kubectl version
```

You should see some output like this:

```
    Client Version: version.Info{Major:"1", Minor:"10",
GitVersion:"v1.10.4", GitCommit:"5ca598b4ba5abb89bb773071ce452e33fb66339d",
GitTreeState:"clean", BuildDate:"2018-06-18T14:14:00Z",
GoVersion:"go1.9.7", Compiler:"gc", Platform:"darwin/amd64"}
    Server Version: version.Info{Major:"1", Minor:"10",
GitVersion:"v1.10.0", GitCommit:"fc32d2f3698e36b93322a3465f63a14e9f0eaead",
```

```
GitTreeState:"clean", BuildDate:"2018-03-26T16:44:10Z",
GoVersion:"go1.9.3", Compiler:"gc", Platform:"linux/amd64"}
```

Your output might show slightly different version numbers, but assuming that you see a version number from both the client and the server, you can connect to the cluster.

If you can't see the server version, or you saw some other error message, skip forward to the *Troubleshooting Minikube* section of this chapter.

Let's start interacting with the cluster with some of the kubectl commands that are going to be useful to us when we interact with our cluster.

The first command that we will explore is the get command. This lets us list basic information about the resources on the cluster. In this case, we are getting a list of all the node resources:

```
kubectl get nodes
NAME        STATUS    AGE     VERSION
minikube    Ready     20h     v1.10.0
```

As you can see, on our Minikube installation, this is not very exciting, as we only have one node. But on larger clusters with many nodes, being able to see this information about all the nodes (or some subset) could be very useful.

The next command will allow us to drill down and look at some more detailed information about a particular resource. Try running the following command against your installation to see what you can discover about the Minikube VM:

```
$ kubectl describe node/minikube
```

As you progress through this book, you will discover that being able to get and describe the various resources that the Kubernetes API exposes will become second nature to you whenever you want to discover what is happening on your cluster and why.

Before we move on, kubectl has one more trick to help us. Try running the following command for a description of each of the resource types available on the cluster and some examples:

```
kubectl describe -h
```

Building Docker containers inside the cluster

You might already have Docker installation on your workstation, but when you are working on an application it can improve your workflow to build your images on the Docker daemon running inside the Minikube VM that hosts your Kubernetes cluster. This means that you can skip pushing your images to a Docker repo before using them in Kubernetes. All you need do is build and tag your images, and then refer to them by name in your Kubernetes resources.

If you already have a Docker installation on your workstation, you should already have the command-line client installed that you need to interact with the Minikube Docker daemon. If you don't, it is quite easy to install, either by installing the Docker package for your platform or, if you just want the command-line tool, downloading the binary and copying it into your path.

To correctly configure the Docker CLI to communicate with the Docker demon inside the minikube VM, minikube provides a command that will return environment variables to configure the client:

```
minikube docker-env
```

On Mac or Linux, you can correctly expand these variables into your current shell environment by running:

```
eval $(minikube docker-env)
```

Try running some `docker` commands to check everything is set up correctly:

```
docker version
```

This should show you the version of Docker running inside the Minikube VM. You might notice that the server version of Docker running in the Minikube VM is a little bit behind the latest version of Docker, since it takes some time for Kubernetes to be tested against new versions of Docker to be considered stable.

Try listing the running containers. You should notice a container running the Kubernetes dashboard, as well as some other services that Kubernetes has launched, such as `kube-dns` and the `addon` manager:

```
docker ps
```

Building and launching a simple application on Minikube

Let's take our first steps to building a simple application on our local minikube cluster and getting it to run.

The first thing we need to do is build a container image for our application. The simplest way to do this is to create a Dockerfile and use the `docker build` command.

Use your favorite text editor to create a file called Dockerfile with the following content:

```
Dockerfile
FROM nginx:alpine
RUN echo "<h1>Hello World</h1>" > /usr/share/nginx/html/index.html
```

To build the application, first ensure your Docker client is pointing to the Docker instance inside the Minikube VM by running:

```
eval $(minikube docker-env)
```

Then use Docker to build the image. In this case, we are tagging the image `hello`, but you could use any tag you wanted:

```
docker build -t hello:v1 .
```

Kubectl has a `run` command that we can use to quickly get a pod running on the Kubernetes cluster. In the background, it creates a Kubernetes deployment resource that ensures that a single instance of our `hello` container runs within a pod (we will learn more about this later):

```
kubectl run hello --image=hello:v1 --image-pull-policy=Never \
--port=80
```

We are setting `--image-pull-policy=Never` here to ensure that Kubernetes uses the local image that we just built, rather than the default of pulling the image from a remote repository, such as Docker Hub.

We can check that our container has started correctly with `kubectl get`:

```
$ kubectl get pods
NAME                      READY    STATUS     RESTARTS    AGE
hello-2033763697-9g7cm    1/1      Running    0           1m
```

Our hello world application was simple enough to set up, but we need some way to access it for our experiment to be considered a success. We can use the kubectl expose command to create a service pointing to the pod in the deployment that was just created:

```
kubectl expose deployment/hello --port=80 --type="NodePort" \
--name=hello
```

We have set the service type to NodePort in this case so that Kubernetes will expose a random port on the Minikube VM so that we can access our service easily. In Chapter 6, *Planning for Production*, we will discuss exposing our applications to the outside world in more detail.

When you create a service of the NodePort type, Kubernetes automatically allocates us a port number for the service to be exposed on. In a multi-node cluster, this port will be opened on every node in the cluster. Since we only have a single node, working out how to access the cluster is a little bit simpler.

First, we need to discover the IP address of the Minikube VM. Luckily, there is a simple command we can run to get this information:

```
minikube ip
192.168.99.100
```

It is more than likely that when the minikube VM started on your machine, it was allocated a different IP address from my own, so make a note of the IP address on your own machine.

Next, in order to discover the port that Kubernetes has exposed our service on, let's use kubectl get on our service:

```
$ kubectl get svc/hello
NAME      CLUSTER-IP    EXTERNAL-IP   PORT(S)       AGE
hello     10.0.0.104    <nodes>       80:32286/TCP  26m
```

You can see, in this case, that Kubernetes has exposed port 80 on our container as port 32286 on our node.

You should now be able to construct a URL that you can visit in your browser to test out the application. In my case, it is `http://192.168.99.100:32286`:

You should be able to visit your application with your web browser

What just happened?

So far, we have managed to build, run, and expose a single container on our Minikube instance. If you are used to using Docker to perform similar tasks, you might notice that although the steps we took were quite simple, there is a little more complexity in getting a simple hello world application like this up and running.

A lot of this has to do with the scope of the tool. Docker provides a simple and easy to use workflow for building and running single containers on a single machine, whereas Kubernetes is, of course, first and foremost a tool designed to manage many containers running across multiple nodes.

In order to understand some of the complexity that Kubernetes introduces, even in this simple example, we are going to explore the ways that Kubernetes is working behind the scenes to keep our application running reliably.

When we executed `kubectl run`, Kubernetes created a new sort of resource: a deployment. A deployment is a higher level abstraction that manages the underlying `ReplicaSet` on our behalf. The advantage of this is that if we want to make changes to our application, Kubernetes can manage rolling out a new configuration to our running application:

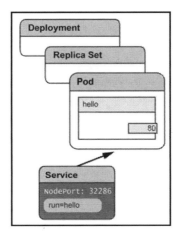

The architecture of our simple Hello application

When we executed kubectl expose, Kubernetes created a service with a label selector that matched the pods under management by the deployment that we referenced.

Rolling out changes

One of the key functions of the deployment resource is to manage the roll-out of new versions of an application. Let's look at an example of how you would do this.

First, let's update the Dockerfile for version 2 of our `Hello World` application:

```
Dockerfile
FROM nginx:alpine
COPY index.html /usr/share/nginx/html/index.html
```

You may have noticed that the HTML we used for version 1 was a little incomplete, so we are using the `COPY` command in the `Dockerfile` to copy an `index.html` file into our container image.

Use your text editor to create an `index.html` file that will be visually distinguishable from version 1. I took the opportunity to add a proper DOCTYPE, and, of course, to use CSS to re-implement the sadly now defunct blink tag! Since this isn't a book about web design, feel free to make whatever changes you want:

index.html
```html
<!DOCTYPE html>
<html>
  <head>
    <style>
      blink { animation: blink 1s steps(1) infinite; }
      @keyframes blink { 50% { color: transparent; } }
    </style>
    <title>Hello World</title>
  </head>
  <body>
    <h1>Hello <blink>1994</blink></h1>
  </body>
</html>
```

Next, use Docker to build your version 2 image:

```
docker build -t hello:v2 .
```

Now we can use kubectl to update the deployment resource to use the new image:

```
kubectl set image deployment/hello hello=hello:v2
```

Wait a few moments for Kubernetes to launch the new pod, and then refresh your browser; you should see your changes.

When we update a deployment, behind the scenes Kubernetes creates a new replica set with the new configuration and handles rolling the new version out. Kubernetes also keeps track of the different configurations you have deployed. This also gives you the ability to roll a deployment back if required:

```
$ kubectl rollout undo deployment/hello
deployment "hello" rolled back
```

Resilience and scaling

Being able to provide services that are resilient to errors and issues in the underlying infrastructure is one of the key reasons why we might want to use Kubernetes to deploy our containerized applications.

We are going to experiment with our `Hello World` deployment to discover how Kubernetes can deal with problems like these.

The first experiment is to see what happens when we deliberately remove the pod where our `hello` container is running.

To do this, we need to find the name of this pod, which we can do with the `kubectl get` command:

```
$ kubectl get pods
NAME                      READY    STATUS     RESTARTS    AGE
hello-2473888519-jc6km    1/1      Running    0           7m
```

On our Minikube cluster, we currently only have one pod running from the one deployment that we have created so far. Once you start to deploy more applications, the output from commands such as kubectl get can get lengthier. We can use the -l flag to pass a label selector to filter down the results. In this case, we would use `kubectl get pods -l run=hello` to show just the pods where the run label is set to `hello`.

Then we can use the `kubectl delete` command to remove the resource. Deleting a pod also terminates the processes running inside of the constituent containers, effectively cleaning up the Docker environment on our node:

```
$ kubectl delete pod/hello-2473888519-jc6km
pod "hello-2473888519-jc6km" delete
```

If we then rerun the `get pods` command, you should notice that the pod we deleted has been replaced by a new one with a new name:

```
$ kubectl get pod
NAME                      READY    STATUS     RESTARTS    AGE
hello-2473888519-1d69q    1/1      Running    0           8s
```

In Kubernetes, we can use replica sets (and deployments) to ensure that pod instances continue to run in our cluster despite unexpected events, be they a failed server, or a fat-fingered admin deleting our pod (as has happened in this case).

You should begin to understand as part of this exercise that a pod is an ephemeral entity. When it is deleted or the node it is running on fails, it is gone forever. Kubernetes ensures that the missing pod is replaced by another, created in its image from the same template. This means that any state that is stored on the local filesystem or in memory, the identity of the pod itself is also lost when a pod inevitably fails and is replaced.

This makes pods well-suited to some kinds of workload where it is not necessary for a state to be stored locally across runs, such as web applications and most batch jobs. If you are building new applications that you intend to deploy to Kubernetes, you will make them easier to manage by delegating the storage of state to an external store, such as a database or a service like Amazon S3.

We will explore features in Kubernetes that allow us to deploy applications that need to store local state and/or maintain a stable identity in *Chapter 9, Storing State*.

One problem you may have noticed when we were testing the abilities of Kubernetes to replace a pod that was removed is that, for a short time, our service became unavailable. For a simple example service running on a single node cluster such as this, perhaps this is not the end of the world. But we do really need a way for our applications to run in a way that minimizes even momentary downtime.

The answer is, of course, to ask Kubernetes to run multiple pin stances for our application, so even if one is lost, a second can take the slack:

```
$ kubectl scale deployment/hello --replicas=2
deployment "hello" scaled
```

If we now check the pods running, we can see a second `hello` pod has joined the party:

```
$ kubectl get pods
NAME                        READY    STATUS     RESTARTS    AGE
hello-2473888519-10p63      1/1      Running    0           1m
hello-2473888519-1d69q      1/1      Running    0           25m
```

Using the dashboard

The Kubernetes dashboard is a web application that runs within your Kubernetes cluster and offers an alternative, more graphical solution, for exploring and monitoring your cluster.

Minikube automatically installs the dashboard and provides a command that will open it in your web browser:

```
$ minikube dashboard
```

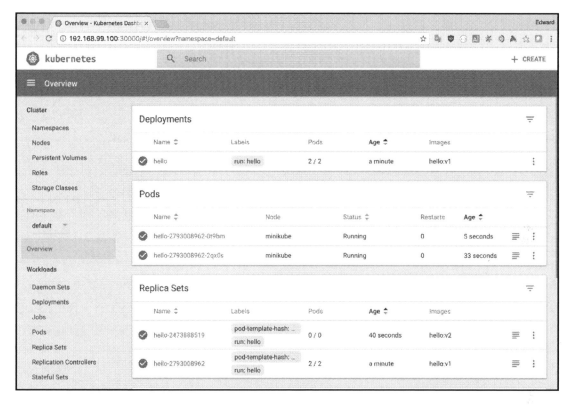

The Kubernetes dashboard

The dashboard interface is very easy to use, and you should begin to notice more than a few similarities with the way that `kubectl` works, since they both allow you to interact with the same underlying API.

The Navigation bar on the left of the screen gives access to screens showing a list of resources of a particular kind. This is similar to the functionality provided by the kubectl get command:

Using the Kubernetes dashboard to list currently running pods

In this view, we can click on the icon that looks like a stack of papers in order to open a log viewer to view the logs captured from standard out in each container in the pod:

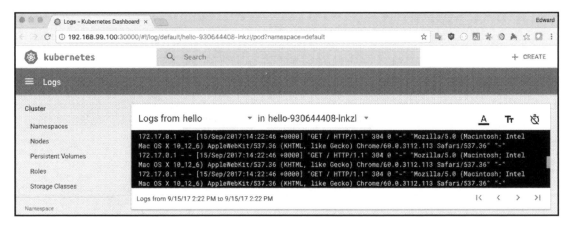

Viewing container logs in the Kubernetes dashboard

Other resources have other options appropriate to their function. For example, Deployments and Replica Sets have a dialog to scale the number of pods up or down.

By clicking on the name of a particular resource, we get a view that shows similar information to `kubectl describe`:

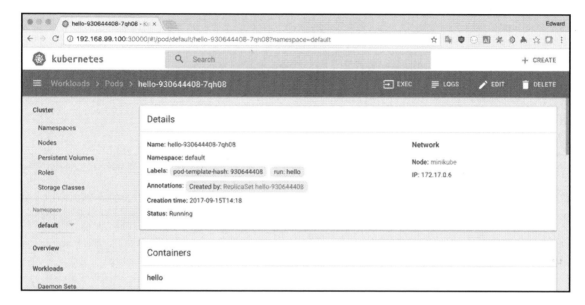

The detail screen provides us quite a lot of information about pods or other resources in Kubernetes:

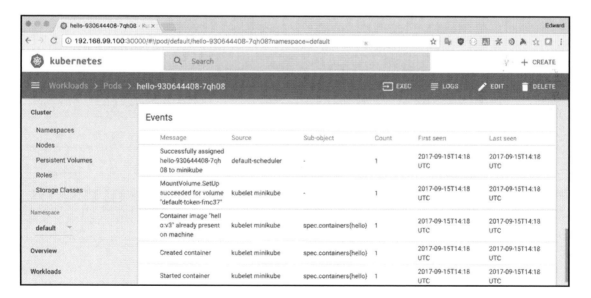

As well as an overview of the configuration and settings for the resources, if you scroll to the bottom of the page, you should be able to see a feed of events. This is very useful if you are trying to debug issues and will highlight any errors or problems with a running resource.

For pods, we get a number of other options for managing and inspecting the container. For example, opening an in-browser terminal by clicking the exec button:

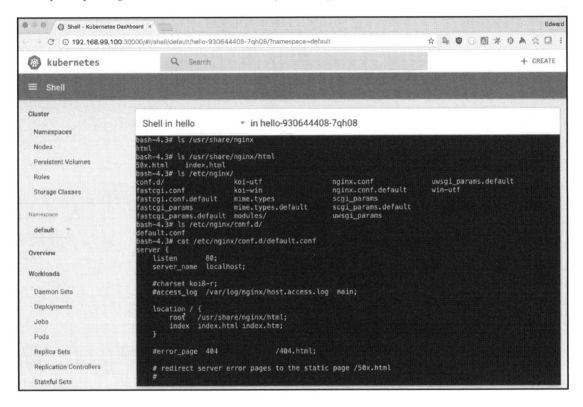

Debugging a container using an interactive shell in the Kubernetes dashboard

Currently, for this feature to work properly, your container needs to have /bin/bash available. This might change in future versions of the dashboard, but for now, to make this work add RUN apk add --no-cache bash to your Dockerfile and deploy the newly built image.

Configuration as code

Throughout this chapter, we have interacted with Kubernetes by using commands provided by kubectl or the Kubernetes dashboard. In practice, I find that these tools are useful for quickly getting a container running in a cluster. When the configuration becomes more complex or I want to be able to deploy the same application to multiple environments, having a configuration file that I can submit to the cluster, and store in a version control system, is very useful.

kubectl and indeed the Kubernetes dashboard, will allow us to submit YAML or JSON formatted configurations for the resources we want to create on the cluster. We are going to take another look at how we would deploy the same Hello World application using YAML-formatted files rather than commands such as kubectl run.

 This Kubernetes configuration is often referred to as a Manifest, and the YAML-or-JSON formatted files as Manifest files.

Let's start by removing the configuration we created with kubectl so we have a clean state to reproduce the same configuration:

```
$ kubectl delete deployment/hello svc/hello
deployment "hello" deleted
service "hello" deleted
```

Let's define a deployment for version 1 of the hello service:

deployment.yaml
```
apiVersion: apps/v1
kind: Deployment
metadata:
  name: hello
spec:
  replicas: 2
  template:
    metadata:
      labels:
        app: hello
    spec:
      containers:
      - name: hello
        image: hello:v1
        ports:
        - containerPort: 80
```

Now we can use `kubectl` to submit the deployment to Kubernetes:

```
$kubectl apply -f deployment.yaml
deployment "hello" created
```

Next, let's do the same for a service:

```
service.yaml
kind: Service
apiVersion: v1
metadata:
  name: hello
spec:
  selector:
    app: hello
  type: NodePort
  ports:
  - protocol: TCP
    port: 80
    targetPort: 80
```

Submit the definition to Kubernetes with `kubectl`:

```
$ kubectl apply -f service.yaml
service "hello" created
```

You can see that while we have sacrificed the speed and simplicity of just running a command to create a deployment, by explicitly specifying the resources we want to create, we gain greater control over exactly how our pods are configured, and we now have this definition in a form that we can check into version control and reliably update.

When it comes to updating a resource, we can make an edit to the file and then use the `kubectl apply` command to update the resource. `kubectl` detects that we are updating an existing resource and updates it to match our configuration. Try editing the image tag in `deployment.yaml` and then re submitting it to the cluster:

```
$ kubectl apply -f deployment.yaml
deployment "hello" configured
```

If we are just making changes to the resource on our local cluster, we might just want to quickly change something without having to edit the file at all. Firstly, as in our previous example, you can use `kubectl set` to update a property. Kubernetes doesn't really care how we created the resource, so everything we did previously is still valid. The other method of making a quick change is with the `kubectl edit` command. Assuming you have the `$EDITOR` environment variable set up correctly with your favorite text editor, you should be able to open YAML for a resource, edit it, and then save while `kubectl` seamlessly updates the resource for you.

Troubleshooting Minikube

One common problem that you might run into when trying to use Minikube is that you might not be able to access the VM because its network overlaps with another network configured on your machine. This can often happen if you are using a corporate VPN, or you connect to another network that configures routes for the `192.168.99.1/24` IP address range used by Minikube by default.

It is simple to start Minikube with an alternative CIDR to be used for the VM. You can choose any private range that you want to use; just check that it won't overlap with other services on your local network:

```
$ minikube start --host-only-cidr=172.16.0.1/24
```

Summary

Well done for making it this far. If you have followed along with the examples in this chapter, you should be well on your way to learning how to use Kubernetes to manage your own applications. You should be able to do the following:

- Use Minikube to set up a single node Kubernetes cluster on your workstation
- Build a simple application container using Docker
- Run a pod on your Minikube cluster
- Declare a Kubernetes configuration using a Manifest file, so you can reproduce your setup
- Set up a service so you can access your application

Reach for the Cloud 3

In this chapter, we are going to learn how to build a Kubernetes cluster that runs on Amazon Web Services from first principles. In order to learn how Kubernetes works, we are going to manually launch the EC2 instances that will form this first cluster and manually install and configure the Kubernetes components.

The cluster that we will build is suitable for you to use when learning about managing Kubernetes and for developing applications that can run on Kubernetes. With these instructions, we are aiming to build the simplest possible cluster that we can deploy to AWS. Of course, this does mean that there are some things that you will want to do differently when building a cluster of mission-critical applications. But don't worry—there are three chapters in Part 3 - Ready for Production where we cover everything you need to know to get your cluster ready for even the most demanding applications.

Running a Kubernetes cluster on AWS costs money. The configuration we will cover in our instructions (a basic cluster with one master and one worker node) at the time of writing will cost around US 75 dollars a month. So if you are just using your cluster for experimentation and learning, remember to shut the instances down when you are finished for the day.

If you have finished with the cluster, terminate the instances and make sure that the EBS volumes have been deleted, because you will pay for these storage volumes even if the instances they are attached to have been stopped.

This chapter is designed to be a learning experience, so read through and type out the commands as you read them. If you have the e-book version of this book, then resist the urge to copy and paste, as you will learn more if you type out the commands and take some time to understand what you are doing. There are tools that will do everything this chapter covers and more just by running one command, but hopefully building your first cluster manually, step by step, will give you some valuable insight into what is required to make a Kubernetes cluster tick.

Cluster architecture

The cluster we are going to set up in this chapter will be formed of two EC2 instances—one that will run all the components for the Kubernetes control plane and another worker node that you can use to run your applications.

Because we start from scratch, this chapter will also lay out one method for isolating your Kubernetes cluster in a private network while allowing you easy access to the machines from your own workstation.

We will achieve this by using an additional instance as a bastion host that will allow incoming SSH connections from the outside world, as shown in the following diagram. If your AWS account already has some infrastructure in place that can achieve this, then feel free to skip this section:

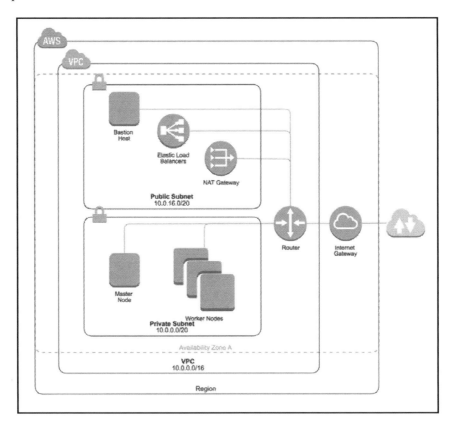

The architecture of the cluster you will set up in this chapter

Creating an AWS account

If you don't already have an AWS account, then head over to `https://aws.amazon.com/` and sign up for one. Before you can create resources in your account, you will need to add a credit card to your account to cover any charges.

When you first sign up for an AWS account, you will be eligible for a free usage tier on some services for the first 12 months. Unfortunately, this free tier doesn't provide quite enough resources to run Kubernetes, but in this chapter, we have optimized our choice of instances for their low cost, so you should be able to follow the examples without spending too much.

Creating an IAM user

When you sign up for an AWS account, the email address and password you choose will be used to log in to the root account. Before you start to interact with AWS, it is a good idea to create an IAM user that you will use to interact with AWS. The advantage of this is that if you wish, you can give each IAM user as much or as little access as they need to AWS services. If you use the root account, you automatically have full access and have no way to manage or revoke privileges. Go through the following steps to set up the account:

1. Once you have logged into the AWS console, go to the **Identity and Access Management** dashboard by clicking on **Services** and typing `IAM` into the search box.
2. From the sidebar, choose **Users** to view the IAM users in your AWS account. If you have only just set up a new account, there won't be any users here—the root account doesn't count as a user.
3. Start the process of setting up a new user account by clicking on the **Add user** button at the top of the screen.

4. Start by choosing a username for your user. Check both boxes to enable **Programmatic access** (so you can use the command-line client) and **AWS Management Console access** so you can log into the web console, as shown in the preceding screenshot:

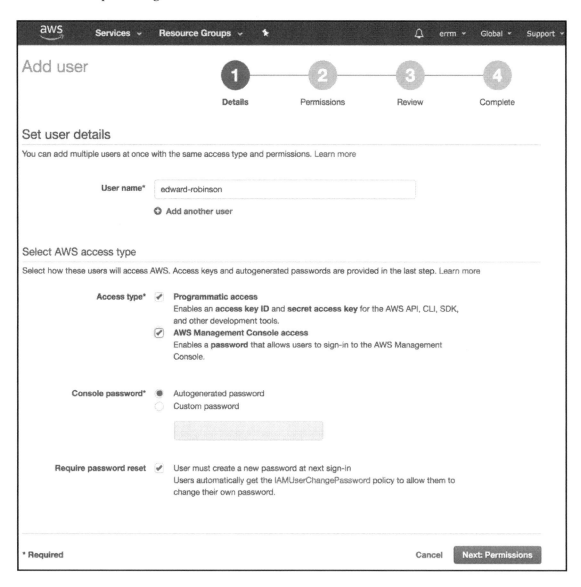

5. On the next screen, you can configure the permissions for your user.
   Choose **Attach existing policies directly**, then choose
   the **AdministratorAccess** policy, as shown in the following screenshot:

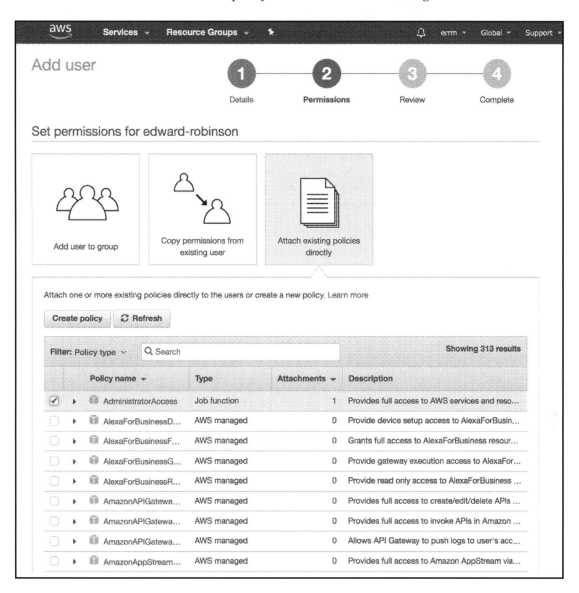

6. Review your settings, then click **Create user**:

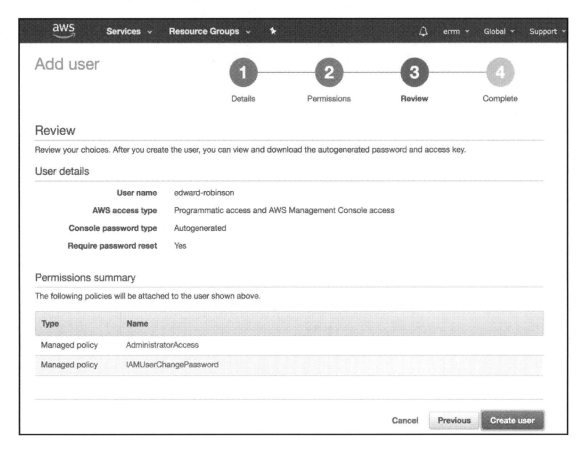

7. Once your user has been created, take a note of the credentials. You will need the **Access key ID** and **Secret access key** shortly to configure the AWS command-line client. Also take a note of the console sign-in link, as this is unique to your AWS account, shown as follows:

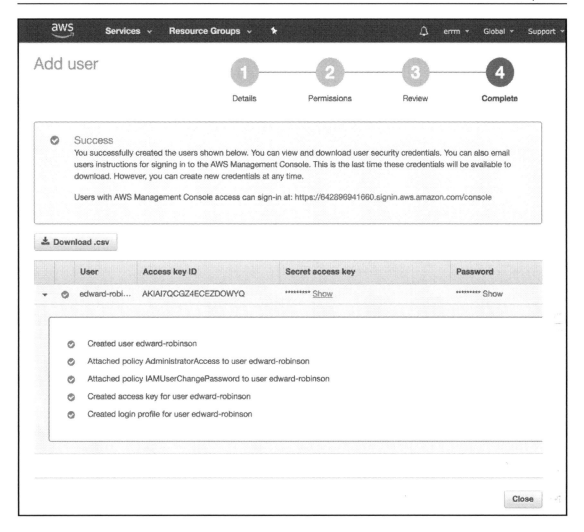

8. Once you have set up an IAM user for yourself, log out of the root account in your browser and check that you can sign back in using your username and password.

You might want to set up two-factor authentication for your AWS account for greater security. Remember that anyone with Administrator access to the account can access or delete any of the resources in your account.

Getting the CLI

You can control AWS using the web console, but your control of AWS will be more precise if you do everything from the command line with the AWS command-line client.

You should follow the instructions provided by AWS to install the command-line client on your system (or by using your systems package manager) using the instructions found at `https://docs.aws.amazon.com/cli/latest/userguide/installing.html`).

Once you have installed the command-line client, run the `aws configure` command to configure the CLI with your credentials. This command will update the `aws config` files in your home directory.

At this stage, you should choose an AWS region for your cluster. For testing and experimentation, it makes sense for you to choose one that is located relatively close to your location. Doing so will improve latency when you access your instances with `ssh` or `connect` to the Kubernetes API.

Setting up a key pair

When we launch an EC2 instance, we want to be able to access it via SSH. We can register a key pair in the EC2 console to allow us to log in once our instance has been launched.

It is possible for us to instruct AWS to generate a key pair for you (that you can then download). But the best practice is to generate a key pair on your workstation and upload the public part to AWS. This ensures that you (and only you) have control of your instance, since the private half of your key will never leave your own machine. To set up the key pair, go through the following steps:

1. You may already have a key pair on your machine that you wish to use. You can check for existing keys by looking in your `.ssh` directory, as follows:

```
$ ls -la ~/.ssh
total 128
drwx------     6 edwardrobinson  staff     192 25 Feb 15:49 .
drwxr-xr-x+ 102 edwardrobinson  staff    3264 25 Feb 15:49 ..
-rw-r--r--     1 edwardrobinson  staff    1759 25 Feb 15:48 config
-rw-------     1 edwardrobinson  staff    3326 25 Feb 15:48 id_rsa
-rw-r--r--     1 edwardrobinson  staff     753 25 Feb 15:48
id_rsa.pub
-rw-r--r--     1 edwardrobinson  staff   53042 25 Feb 15:48
known_hosts
```

2. In this example, you can see that I have one key pair in my `.ssh` directory—the private key has the default name of `id_rsa` and the public key is called `id_rsa.pub`.

3. If you don't already have a key pair set up, or if you want to create a fresh one, then you can use the `ssh-keygen` command to create a new one, as follows:

```
$ ssh-keygen -t rsa -b 4096 -C "email@example.com"
Generating public/private rsa key pair.
```

4. This command creates a new key pair using your email address as a label.

5. Next, choose where to save the new key pair. If you don't already have a key pair, just press *Enter* to write it to the default location as follows:

```
Enter file in which to save the key
(/home/edwardrobinson/.ssh/id_rsa):
```

6. Next, you will be asked for a passphrase (password). If you just press *Enter*, then the key will be created without any password protection, as shown in the following command. If you choose a password, make sure that you remember it or store it securely, as you won't be able to use your SSH key (or access your instances) without it.

```
Enter passphrase (empty for no passphrase):
Enter same passphrase again:
Your identification has been saved in
/home/edwardrobinson/.ssh/id_rsa.
Your public key has been saved in /home/edwardrobinson/.ssh/id_rsa.
The key fingerprint is:
SHA256:noWDFhnDxcvF17DGi6EnF9EM5yeRMfGX1wt85wnbxxQ
email@example.com
```

7. Once you have an SSH key pair on your machine, you can go about importing it into your AWS account. Remember that you only need to import the public part of your key pair. This will be in a file that ends with the `.pub` extension.

8. From the AWS EC2 console (click on **Services** and then search for **EC2**), choose **Key Pairs** from the menu on the left of the screen, as shown in the following screenshot:

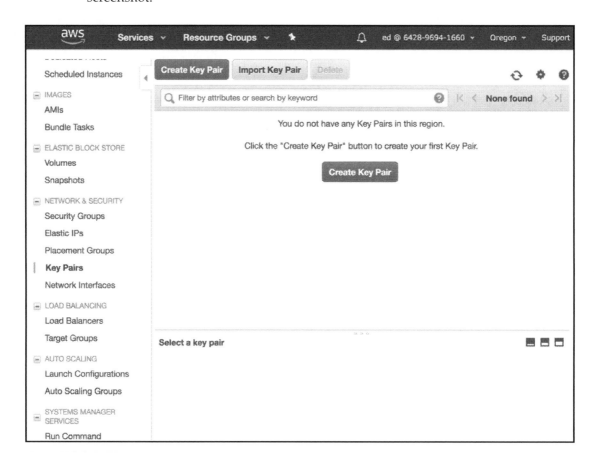

9. From this screen, choose **Import Key Pair** to bring up a dialog where you can upload your key pair, as shown in the following screenshot:

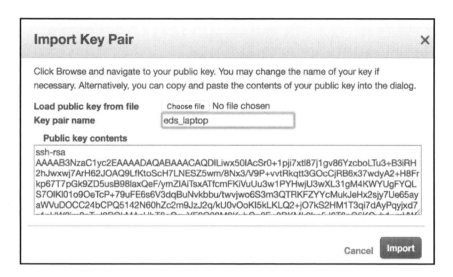

10. Choose a name that will identify your key pair within AWS (I chose `eds_laptop`). Then, either navigate to your key's location or just paste its text into the large text box, and then click **Import**. Once you have imported your key, you should see it listed on the **Key Pairs** page.

If you are using AWS in more than one region, you will need to import a key pair in each region that you want to launch instances in.

Preparing the network

We will set up a new VPC in your AWS account. A VPC, or virtual private cloud, allows us to have a private network that is isolated from all the other users of EC2 and the internet that we can launch instances onto.

It provides a secure foundation that we can use to build a secure network for our cluster, as shown in the following command:

```
$ VPC_ID=$(aws ec2 create-vpc --cidr-block 10.0.0.0/16 --query "Vpc.VpcId"
--output text)
```

The `VpcId` will be unique to your account, so I am going to set a shell variable that I can use to refer to it whenever we need. You can do the same with the `VpcId` from your account, or you might prefer to just type it out each time you need it.

The rest of the steps in this chapter follow this pattern, but if you don't understand what is happening, don't be afraid to look at the shell variables and correlate the IDs with the resources in the AWS console, as follows:

```
$ echo $VPC_ID
```

Kubernetes names your instances based on the internal DNS hostnames that AWS assigns to them. If we enable DNS support in the VPC, then we will be able to resolve these hostnames when using the DNS server provided inside the VPC, as follows:

```
$ aws ec2 modify-vpc-attribute \
    --enable-dns-support \
    --vpc-id $VPC_ID
$ aws ec2 modify-vpc-attribute \
    --enable-dns-hostnames \
    --vpc-id $VPC_ID
```

Kubernetes makes extensive use of AWS resource tags, so it knows which resources it can use and which resources are managed by Kubernetes. The key for these tags is `kubernetes.io/cluster/<cluster_name>`. For resources that might be shared between several distinct clusters, we use the `shared` value. This means that Kubernetes can make use of them, but won't ever remove them from your account.

We would use this for resources such as VPCs. Resources where the life cycle is fully managed by Kubernetes have a tag value of `owned` and may be deleted by Kubernetes if they are no longer required. Kubernetes typically creates these tags automatically when it creates resources such as instances in an autoscaling group, EBS volumes, or load balancers.

 I like to name the clusters I create after famous people from the history of computer science. The cluster I created for this chapter is named after Grace Hopper, who designed the COBOL programming language.

Let's add a tag to our new VPC so that Kubernetes will be able to use it, as shown in the following command:

```
aws ec2 create-tags \
--resources $VPC_ID \
--tags Key=Name,Value=hopper \
  Key=kubernetes.io/cluster/hopper,Value=shared
```

When we created our VPC, a main route table was automatically created. We will use this for routing in our private subnet. Let's grab the ID to use later, as shown in the following command:

```
$ PRIVATE_ROUTE_TABLE_ID=$(aws ec2 describe-route-tables \
    --filters Name=vpc-id,Values=$VPC_ID \
    --query "RouteTables[0].RouteTableId" \
    --output=text)
```

Now we will add a second route table to manage routing for the public subnets in our VPC, as follows:

```
$ PUBLIC_ROUTE_TABLE_ID=$(aws ec2 create-route-table \
  --vpc-id $VPC_ID \
  --query "RouteTable.RouteTableId" --output text)
```

Now we will give the route tables names so we can keep track of them later:

```
$ aws ec2 create-tags \
  --resources $PUBLIC_ROUTE_TABLE_ID \
  --tags Key=Name,Value=hopper-public
$ aws ec2 create-tags \
  --resources $PRIVATE_ROUTE_TABLE_ID \
  --tags Key=Name,Value=hopper-private
```

Next, we are going to create two subnets for our cluster to use. Because I am creating my cluster in the `eu-west-1` region (Ireland), I am going to create these subnets in the `eu-west-1a` subnet. You should choose an availability zone for your cluster from the region you are using by running `aws ec2 describe-availability-zones`. In Part 3, we will learn how to create high-availability clusters that span multiple availability zones.

Let's start by creating a subnet for instances that will only be accessible from within our private network. We are going to use a `/20 netmask` on the CIDR block, as shown in the following command; with this, AWS will give us 4089 IP addresses that will be available to be assigned to our EC2 instances and to pods launched by Kubernetes:

```
$ PRIVATE_SUBNET_ID=$(aws ec2 create-subnet \
  --vpc-id $VPC_ID \
  --availability-zone eu-west-1a \
  --cidr-block 10.0.0.0/20 --query "Subnet.SubnetId" \
  --output text)
$ aws ec2 create-tags \
  --resources $PRIVATE_SUBNET_ID \
  --tags Key=Name,Value=hopper-private-1a \
    Key=kubernetes.io/cluster/hopper,Value=owned \
    Key=kubernetes.io/role/internal-elb,Value=1
```

Next, let's add another subnet to the same availability zone, as shown in the following command. We will use this subnet for instances that need to be accessible from the internet, such as public load balancers and bastion hosts:

```
$ PUBLIC_SUBNET_ID=$(aws ec2 create-subnet \
  --vpc-id $VPC_ID \
  --availability-zone eu-west-1a \
  --cidr-block 10.0.16.0/20 --query "Subnet.SubnetId" \
  --output text)
$ aws ec2 create-tags \
  --resources $PUBLIC_SUBNET_ID \
  --tags Key=Name,Value=hopper-public-1a \
    Key=kubernetes.io/cluster/hopper,Value=owned \
    Key=kubernetes.io/role/elb,Value=1
```

Next, we should associate this subnet with the public route table, as follows:

```
$ aws ec2 associate-route-table \
  --subnet-id $PUBLIC_SUBNET_ID \
  --route-table-id $PUBLIC_ROUTE_TABLE_ID
```

In order for the instances in our public subnet to communicate with the internet, we will create an internet gateway, attach it to our VPC, and then add a route to the route table, routing traffic bound for the internet to the gateway, as shown in the following command:

```
$ INTERNET_GATEWAY_ID=$(aws ec2 create-internet-gateway \
    --query "InternetGateway.InternetGatewayId" --output text)
$ aws ec2 attach-internet-gateway \
    --internet-gateway-id $INTERNET_GATEWAY_ID \
    --vpc-id $VPC_ID
$ aws ec2 create-route \
    --route-table-id $PUBLIC_ROUTE_TABLE_ID \
    --destination-cidr-block 0.0.0.0/0 \
    --gateway-id $INTERNET_GATEWAY_ID
```

In order to configure the instances in the private subnet, we will need them to be able to make outbound connections to the internet in order to install software packages and so on. To make this possible, we will add a NAT gateway to the public subnet and then add a route to the private route table for internet-bound traffic, as follows:

```
$ NAT_GATEWAY_ALLOCATION_ID=$(aws ec2 allocate-address \
    --domain vpc --query AllocationId --output text)
$ NAT_GATEWAY_ID=$(aws ec2 create-nat-gateway \
    --subnet-id $PUBLIC_SUBNET_ID \
    --allocation-id $NAT_GATEWAY_ALLOCATION_ID \
    --query NatGateway.NatGatewayId --output text)
```

At this stage, you may have to wait a few moments for the NAT gateway to be created before creating the route, as shown in the following command:

```
$ aws ec2 create-route \
    --route-table-id $PRIVATE_ROUTE_TABLE_ID \
    --destination-cidr-block 0.0.0.0/0 \
    --nat-gateway-id $NAT_GATEWAY_ID
```

Setting up a bastion

We will use the first host we are going to launch as a bastion host that will allow us to connect to other servers that are only accessible from within the private side of our VPC network.

We will be creating a security group to allow SSH traffic to this instance. We will use the `aws ec2 create-security-group` command to create a security group for our bastion host, as shown in the following command. A security group is an abstraction that AWS provides in order to group related firewall rules together and apply them to groups of hosts:

```
$ BASTION_SG_ID=$(aws ec2 create-security-group \
    --group-name ssh-bastion \
    --description "SSH Bastion Hosts" \
    --vpc-id $VPC_ID \
    --query GroupId --output text)
```

Once we have created a security group, we can attach a rule to it to allow SSH ingress on port 22, as shown in the following command. This will allow you to access your host with an SSH client. Here, I am allowing ingress from the CIDR range 0.0.0.0/0, but if your internet connection has a stable IP address, you might want to limit access to just your own IP:

```
$ aws ec2 authorize-security-group-ingress \
    --group-id $BASTION_SG_ID \
    --protocol tcp \
    --port 22 \
    --cidr 0.0.0.0/0
```

Now that we have set up the security group for the bastion host, we can go about launching our first EC2 instance. In this chapter, I will be using Ubuntu Linux (a popular Linux distribution). Before we can launch the instance, we will need to discover the ID of the AMI (Amazon machine image) for the operating system we want to use.

The Ubuntu project regularly publishes updated images to their AWS account that can be used to launch EC2 instances. We can run the following command to discover the ID of the image that we require:

```
$ UBUNTU_AMI_ID=$(aws ec2 describe-images --owners 099720109477 \
   --filters Name=root-device-type,Values=ebs \
           Name=architecture,Values=x86_64 \
           Name=name,Values='*hvm-ssd/ubuntu-xenial-16.04*' \
   --query "sort_by(Images, &Name)[-1].ImageId" --output text)
```

We are going to use a `t2.micro` instance for the bastion host (as shown in the following command), as the usage for this instance type is included in the AWS free tier, so you won't have to pay for it for the first 12 months after you set up your AWS account:

```
$ BASTION_ID=$(aws ec2 run-instances \
   --image-id $UBUNTU_AMI_ID \
   --instance-type t2.micro \
   --key-name eds_laptop \
   --security-group-ids $BASTION_SG_ID \
   --subnet-id $PUBLIC_SUBNET_ID \
   --associate-public-ip-address \
   --query "Instances[0].InstanceId" \
   --output text)
```

Note that we are passing the ID of the subnet we chose to use, the ID of the security group we just created, and the name of the key pair we uploaded.

Next, let's update the instance with a `Name` tag so we can recognize it when looking at the EC2 console, as shown in the following command:

```
$ aws ec2 create-tags \
   --resources $BASTION_ID \
   --tags Key=Name,Value=ssh-bastion
```

Once the instance has launched, you should be able to run the `aws ec2 describe-instances` command to discover the public IP address of your new instance, as follows:

```
$ BASTION_IP=$(aws ec2 describe-instances \
   --instance-ids $BASTION_ID \
   --query "Reservations[0].Instances[0].PublicIpAddress" \
   --output text)
```

You should now be able to access the instance with SSH, as follows:

```
$ ssh ubuntu@$BASTION_IP
```

As you log in, you should see a message like the following:

```
Welcome to Ubuntu 16.04.3 LTS (GNU/Linux 4.4.0-1052-aws x86_64)
 * Documentation:  https://help.ubuntu.com
 * Management:     https://landscape.canonical.com
 * Support:        https://ubuntu.com/advantage
  Get cloud support with Ubuntu Advantage Cloud Guest:
        http://www.ubuntu.com/business/services/cloud
0 packages can be updated.
0 updates are security updates.

To run a command as administrator (user "root"), use "sudo <command>".
See "man sudo_root" for details.
ubuntu@ip-10-0-26-86:~$
```

> If you saved your key pair as something other than the default
> ~/.ssh/id_rsa, you can pass the path to your key using the -i flag, as
> follows:
>
> ssh -i ~/.ssh/id_aws_rsa ubuntu@$BASTION_IP
>
> As an alternative, you can add the key to your SSH agent first by running
> the following:
>
> ssh-add ~/.ssh/id_aws_rsa

sshuttle

It is possible to forward traffic from your workstation to the private network by just using SSH. However, we can make accessing servers via the bastion instance much more convenient by using the sshuttle tool.

It is simple to install sshuttle on your workstation.

You can install it on macOS using Homebrew, as follows:

```
brew install sshuttle
```

You can also install it on Linux (if you have Python installed), as follows:

```
pip install sshuttle
```

To transparently proxy traffic to the instances inside the private network, we can run the following command:

```
$ sshuttle -r ubuntu@$BASTION_IP 10.0.0.0/16 --dns
[local sudo] Password:
client: Connected.
```

Firstly, we pass the SSH login details of our `ubuntu@$BASTION_IP` bastion instance, followed by the CIDR of our VPC (so that only traffic destined for the private network passes over the tunnel); this can be found by running `aws ec2 describe-vpcs`. Finally, we pass the `--dns` flag so that DNS queries on your workstation will be resolved by the DNS servers of the remote instance.

Using `sshuttle` requires you to enter your local sudo password in order to set up its proxy server.

 You might want to run `sshuttle` in a separate terminal or in the background so that you still have access to the shell variables we have been using.

We can validate that this setup is working correctly by trying to log in to our instance through its private DNS name, as follows:

```
$ aws ec2 describe-instances \
  --instance-ids $BASTION_ID \
  --query "Reservations[0].Instances[0].PrivateDnsName"
"ip-10-0-21-138.eu-west-1.compute.internal"
$ ssh ubuntu@ip-10-0-21-138.eu-west-1.compute.internal
```

This tests whether you can resolve a DNS entry from the private DNS provided by AWS to instances running within your VPC, and whether the private IP address now returned by that query is reachable.

If you have any difficulties, check `sshuttle` for any connection errors and ensure that you have remembered to enable DNS support in your VPC.

Instance profiles

In order for Kubernetes to make use of its integrations with the AWS cloud APIs, we need to set up IAM instance profiles. An instance profile is a way for the Kubernetes software to authenticate with the AWS API, and for us to assign fine-grained permissions on the actions that Kubernetes can take.

It can be confusing to learn all of the permissions that Kubernetes requires to function correctly. You could just set up instance profiles that allow full access to AWS, but this would be at the expense of security best practice.

Whenever we assign security permissions, we should be aiming to grant just enough permissions for our software to function correctly. To this end, I have collated a set of minimal IAM policies that will allow our cluster to function correctly, without giving excess permissions away.

You can view these policies at `https://github.com/errm/k8s-iam-policies`, where I have documented each policy with a brief description of its purpose.

The repository includes a simple shell script that we can use to create an IAM instance profile for the master and worker nodes in our cluster, as follows:

```
$ curl
https://raw.githubusercontent.com/errm/k8s-iam-policies/master/setup.sh -o
setup.sh
$ sh -e setup.sh
  {
      "InstanceProfile": {
          "Path": "/",
          "InstanceProfileName": "K8sMaster",
          "InstanceProfileId": "AIPAJ7YTS67QLILBZUQYE",
          "Arn": "arn:aws:iam::642896941660:instance-profile/K8sMaster",
          "CreateDate": "2018-02-26T19:06:19.831Z",
          "Roles": []
      }
  }
  {
      "InstanceProfile": {
          "Path": "/",
          "InstanceProfileName": "K8sNode",
          "InstanceProfileId": "AIPAJ27KNVOKTLZV7DDA4",
          "Arn": "arn:aws:iam::642896941660:instance-profile/K8sNode",
          "CreateDate": "2018-02-26T19:06:25.282Z",
          "Roles": []
      }
  }
```

Kubernetes software

We are going to launch an instance in which we will install all of the software that the different nodes that make up our cluster will need. We will then create an AMI, or Amazon machine image, that we can use to launch the nodes on our cluster.

First, we create a security group for this instance, as follows:

```
$ K8S_AMI_SG_ID=$(aws ec2 create-security-group \
    --group-name k8s-ami \
    --description "Kubernetes AMI Instances" \
    --vpc-id $VPC_ID \
    --query GroupId \
    --output text)
```

We will need to be able to access this instance from our bastion host in order to log in and install software, so let's add a rule to allow SSH traffic on port 22 from instances in the ssh-bastion security group, as follows:

```
$ aws ec2 authorize-security-group-ingress \
    --group-id $K8S_AMI_SG_ID \
    --protocol tcp \
    --port 22 \
    --source-group $BASTION_SG_ID
```

We are just using a t2.mico instance here since we don't need a very powerful instance just to install packages, as shown in the following command:

```
$ K8S_AMI_INSTANCE_ID=$(aws ec2 run-instances \
    --subnet-id $PRIVATE_SUBNET_ID \
    --image-id $UBUNTU_AMI_ID \
    --instance-type t2.micro \
    --key-name eds_laptop \
    --security-group-ids $K8S_AMI_SG_ID \
    --query "Instances[0].InstanceId" \
    --output text)
```

We add a Name tag so we can identify the instance later if we need, as follows:

```
$ aws ec2 create-tags \
    --resources $K8S_AMI_INSTANCE_ID \
    --tags Key=Name,Value=kubernetes-node-ami
```

Grab the IP address of the instance, as follows:

```
$ K8S_AMI_IP=$(aws ec2 describe-instances \
    --instance-ids $K8S_AMI_INSTANCE_ID \
    --query "Reservations[0].Instances[0].PrivateIpAddress" \
    --output text)
```

Then log in with `ssh`, as follows:

```
$ ssh ubuntu@$K8S_AMI_IP
```

Now we are ready to start configuring the instance with the software and configuration that all of the nodes in our cluster will need. Start by synchronizing the apt repositories, as follows:

```
$ sudo apt-get update
```

Docker

Kubernetes can work with a number of container runtimes, but Docker is still the most widely used.

Before we install Docker, we will add a `systemd` drop-in config file to the Docker service, as follows:

```
/etc/systemd/system/docker.service.d/10-iptables.conf
[Service]
ExecStartPost=/sbin/iptables -P FORWARD ACCEPT
```

In order for our Kubernetes pods to be accessible to other instances in the cluster, we need to set the default policy for the `iptables FORWARD` chain as shown in the following command; otherwise, Docker will set this to `DROP` and traffic for Kubernetes services will be dropped:

```
$ sudo mkdir -p /etc/systemd/system/docker.service.d/
$ printf "[Service]\nExecStartPost=/sbin/iptables -P FORWARD ACCEPT" |
sudo tee /etc/systemd/system/docker.service.d/10-iptables.conf
```

Kubernetes will work well with the version of Docker that is included in the Ubuntu repositories, so we can install it simply by installing the `docker.io` package, as follows:

```
$ sudo apt-get install -y docker.io
```

Check that Docker is installed by running the following:

```
$ sudo docker version
```

Installing Kubeadm

Next, we will install the packages that we need to set up a Kubernetes control plane on this host. These packages are described in the following list:

- `kubelet`: The node agent that Kubernetes uses to control the container runtime. This is used to run all the other components of the control plane within Docker containers.
- `kubeadm`: This utility is responsible for bootstrapping a Kubernetes cluster.
- `kubectl`: The Kubernetes command-line client, which will allow us to interact with the Kubernetes API server.

First, add the signing key for the apt repository that hosts the Kubernetes packages, as follows:

```
$ curl -s https://packages.cloud.google.com/apt/doc/apt-key.gpg | sudo apt-
key add -
OK
```

Next add the Kubernetes apt repository, as follows:

```
$ sudo apt-add-repository 'deb http://apt.kubernetes.io/ kubernetes-xenial
main'
```

Then, resynchronize the package indexes, as follows:

```
$ sudo apt-get update
```

Then, install the required packages, as follows:

```
$ sudo apt-get install -y kubelet kubeadm kubectl
```

This will install the latest version of the packages. If you want to pin to a specific version of Kubernetes, try running `apt-cache madison kubeadm` to see the different versions available.

I have prepared this chapter using Kubernetes 1.10. If, you wanted to install the most recent release of Kubernetes 1.10, you could run the following command:

```
sudo apt-get install kubeadm=1.10.* kubectl=1.10.*
kubelet=1.10.*
```

Building an AMI

Now that we are done with installing packages on this instance, we can shut it down, as follows:

```
$ sudo shutdown -h now
Connection to 10.0.13.93 closed by remote host.
Connection to 10.0.13.93 closed.
```

We can use the `create-image` command to instruct AWS to snapshot the root volume of our instance and use it to produce an AMI, as shown in the following command (you might need to wait a few moments for the instance to fully stop before running the command):

```
$ K8S_AMI_ID=$(aws ec2 create-image \
      --name k8s-1.10.3-001 \
      --instance-id $K8S_AMI_INSTANCE_ID \
      --description "Kubernetes v1.10.3" \
      --query ImageId \
    --output text)
```

It can take a few minutes for the image to become available for you to use, but you can check on its status with the `describe-images` command, as follows:

```
aws ec2 describe-images \
      --image-ids $K8S_AMI_ID \
      --query "Images[0].State"
```

While the image is being built, you will see `pending`, but once it is ready to use the state will have changed to `available`.

Bootstrapping the cluster

Now we can launch an instance for Kubernetes control plane components. First, we will create a security group for this new instance, as follows:

```
$ K8S_MASTER_SG_ID=$(aws ec2 create-security-group \
      --group-name k8s-master \
      --description "Kubernetes Master Hosts" \
      --vpc-id $VPC_ID \
      --query GroupId \
      --output text)
```

We will need to be able to access this instance from our bastion host in order to log in and configure the cluster. We will add a rule to allow SSH traffic on port 22 from instances in the ssh-bastion security group, as follows:

```
$ aws ec2 authorize-security-group-ingress \
    --group-id $K8S_MASTER_SG_ID \
    --protocol tcp \
    --port 22 \
    --source-group $BASTION_SG_ID
```

Now we can launch the instance, as follows:

```
$ K8S_MASTER_INSTANCE_ID=$(aws ec2 run-instances \
    --private-ip-address 10.0.0.10 \
    --subnet-id $PRIVATE_SUBNET_ID \
    --image-id $K8S_AMI_ID \
    --instance-type t2.medium \
    --key-name eds_laptop \
    --security-group-ids $K8S_MASTER_SG_ID \
    --credit-specification CpuCredits=unlimited \
    --iam-instance-profile Name=K8sMaster \
    --query "Instances[0].InstanceId" \
    --output text)
```

We should give the instance a name, and to ensure that Kubernetes can associate all of the resources with our cluster, we will also add the KubernetesCluster tag with a name for this cluster, as follows:

```
$ aws ec2 create-tags \
  --resources $K8S_MASTER_INSTANCE_ID \
  --tags Key=Name,Value=hopper-k8s-master \
    Key=kubernetes.io/cluster/hopper,Value=owned
$ ssh ubuntu@10.0.0.10
```

To ensure that all the Kubernetes components use the same name, we should set the hostname to match the name given by the AWS metadata service, as shown in the following command. This is because the name from the metadata service is used by components that have the AWS cloud provider enabled:

```
$ sudo hostnamectl set-hostname $(curl
http://169.254.169.254/latest/meta-data/hostname)
$ hostnamectl status
    Static hostname: ip-10-0-0-10.eu-west-1.compute.internal
```

To correctly configure the kubelet to use the AWS cloud provider, we create a `systemd` drop-in file to pass some extra arguments to the kubelet, as follows:

```
/etc/systemd/system/kubelet.service.d/20-aws.conf
[Service]
Environment="KUBELET_EXTRA_ARGS=--cloud-provider=aws --node ip=10.0.0.10"
$ printf '[Service]\nEnvironment="KUBELET_EXTRA_ARGS=--cloud-provider=aws -
-node-ip=10.0.0.10"' | sudo tee /etc/systemd/system/kubelet.service.d/20-
aws.conf
```

Once you have added this file, reload the `systemd` configuration, as follows:

```
$ sudo systemctl daemon-reload
$ sudo systemctl restart kubelet
```

We need to provide `kubeadm` with a configuration file in order to enable the AWS cloud provider on each of the components that it will launch. Here, we also set `tokenTTL` to 0, as shown in the following command; this means that the token that is issued to allow worker nodes to join the cluster won't expire. This is important, as we plan to manage our workers with an autoscaling group, and new nodes could join the group after a while:

```
kubeadm.config
apiVersion: kubeadm.k8s.io/v1alpha1
kind: MasterConfiguration
cloudProvider: aws
tokenTTL: "0"
```

Now we just need to run the following command to bootstrap the master:

```
$ sudo kubeadm init --config=kubeadm.config
[init] Using Kubernetes version: v1.10.3 .. .
. . .
. . .
Your Kubernetes master has initialized successfully!
. . .
```

You should see the preceding message followed by some instructions to set up the rest of the cluster. Make a note of the `kubeadm join` command as we will need it to set up the worker node(s).

We can check that the API server is functioning correctly by following the instructions given by `kubeadm` to set up `kubectl` on the host, as shown in the following command:

```
$ mkdir -p $HOME/.kube
$ sudo cp -i /etc/kubernetes/admin.conf $HOME/.kube/config
$ sudo chown $(id -u):$(id -g) $HOME/.kube/config
```

Try running the `kubectl` version. If `kubectl` can correctly connect to the host, then you should be able to see the version of the Kubernetes software for the client (`kubectl`) and on the server, as shown in the following command:

```
$ kubectl version
Client Version: version.Info{Major:"1", Minor:"9", GitVersion:"v1.9.3",
GitCommit:"d2835416544f298c919e2ead3be3d0864b52323b", GitTreeState:"clean",
BuildDate:"2018-02-07T12:22:21Z", GoVersion:"go1.9.2", Compiler:"gc",
Platform:"linux/amd64"}
Server Version: version.Info{Major:"1", Minor:"9", GitVersion:"v1.9.3",
GitCommit:"d2835416544f298c919e2ead3be3d0864b52323b", GitTreeState:"clean",
BuildDate:"2018-02-07T11:55:20Z", GoVersion:"go1.9.2", Compiler:"gc",
Platform:"linux/amd64"}
```

What just happened?

So that was easy right? We got the Kubernetes control plane up and running by running one command.

The `kubeadm` command is a fantastic tool because it takes a lot of the guesswork out of correctly configuring Kubernetes. But let's take a brief intermission from setting up our cluster and dig a little bit deeper to discover what actually just happened.

Looking though the output from the `kubeadm` command should give us some clues.

The first thing that `kubeadm` did was to establish a private key infrastructure. If you take a look at the `/etc/kubernetes/pki` directory, you can see a number of `ssl` certificates and private keys, as well as a certificate authority that was used to sign each key pair. Now, when we add worker nodes to the cluster, they will be able to establish secure communication between the kubelet and the `apiserver`.

Next, `kubedam` wrote static pod manifests to the `/etc/kubernetes/manifests/` directory. These manifests are just like the pod definitions that you would submit to the Kubernetes API sever to run your own applications, but since the API server has not yet started, the definition is read directly from the disk by the `kubelet`.

The `kubelet` is configured to read these static pod manifests in a `systemd dropin` that `kubeadm` creates at `etc/systemd/system/kubelet.service.d/10-kubeadm.conf`. You can see the following flag among the other configurations:

```
--pod-manifest-path=/etc/kubernetes/manifests
```

If you look in `/etc/kubernetes/manifests/`, you will see Kubernetes pod specifications for each of the components that form the control plane, as described in the following list:

- `etcd.yaml`: The key value store that stores the state of the API server
- `kube-apiserver.yaml`: The API server
- `kube-controller-manager.yaml`: The controller manager
- `kube-scheduler.yaml`: The scheduler

Finally, once the API server has started, `kubeadm` submits two add-ons to the API, as described in the following list:

- `kube-proxy`: This is the process that configures iptables on each node to make the service IPs route correctly. It is run on each node with a DaemonSet. You can look at this configuration by running `kubectl -n kube-system describe ds kube-proxy`.
- `kube-dns`: This process provides the DNS server that can be used by applications running on the cluster for service discovery. Note that it will not start running correctly until you have configured a pod network for your cluster. You can view the configuration for `kube-dns` by running `kubectl -n kube-system describe deployment kube-dns`.

> You could try using `kubectl` to explore the different components that make up the Kubernetes control plane. Try running the following commands:
> ```
> $ kubectl -n kube-system get pods
> $ kubectl -n kube-system describe pods
> $ kubectl -n kube-system get daemonsets
> $ kubectl -n kube-system get deployments
> Before you continue with the next section, log out of the
> master instance, as follows:
> $ exit
> logout
> Connection to 10.0.0.10 closed.
> ```

Access the API from your workstation

It is convenient to be able to access the Kubernetes API server via `kubectl` on your workstation. It means that you can submit any manifests that you may have been developing to your cluster running on AWS.

We need to allow traffic from the bastion server to access the API server. Let's add a rule to the `K8S-MASTER` security group to allow this traffic, as follows:

```
$ aws ec2 authorize-security-group-ingress \
    --group-id $K8S_MASTER_SG_ID \
    --protocol tcp \
    --port 6443 \
    --source-group $BASTION_SG_ID
```

If you haven't already installed kubectl on your workstation, turn back to Chapter 2, *Start Your Engines*, to learn how.

Now we can copy the `kubeconfig` file from the master instance.

If you do not already have any clusters configured in your local `~/.kube/config` file, you can copy the file from the master, as follows:

```
$ scp ubuntu@10.0.0.10:~/.kube/config ~/.kube/config
```

> If you already have a cluster configured (for example, minikube), then you may wish to merge the config for your new cluster, or use another file and pass its location to `kubectl` with the `--kubeconfig` flag, or in the `KUBECONFIG` environment variable.

Check that you can connect to the API server using your local `kubectl`, as follows:

```
$ kubectl get nodes
NAME              STATUS      AGE     VERSION
ip-10-0-9-172...  NotReady    5m      v1.9.3
```

If you have any problem connecting, check that `sshuttle` is still running, and that you have correctly allowed access from the bastion host to the k8s-master security group.

Setting up pod networking

You may have noticed that, when running `kubectl get nodes`, the `NodeStatus` is `NotReady`. This is because the cluster we have bootstrapped is missing one essential component—the network infrastructure that will allow the pods running on our cluster to communicate with one another.

The network model of a Kubernetes cluster is somewhat different from that of a standard Docker installation. There are many implementations of networking infrastructure that can provide cluster networking for Kubernetes, but they all have some key attributes in common, as shown in the following list:

- Each pod is assigned its own IP address
- Each pod can communicate with any other pod in the cluster without NAT (not withstanding additional security policies)
- The internal network that the software running inside a pod sees is identical to the pod network seen by other pods in the cluster—that is, it sees that the IP address is the same and that no port mapping takes place

This networking arrangement is much simpler (for users of the cluster) than Docker's standard networking scheme of mapping internal ports in the container to other ports on the host.

It does, however, require some integration between the network infrastructure and Kubernetes. Kubernetes manages this integration though an interface called the **container network interface** (**CNI**). It is simple to deploy a **CNI** plugin to each node of your cluster with a Kubernetes DaemonSet.

If you want to learn more about Kubernetes cluster networking, I recommend reading the comprehensive documentation of the underlying concepts at `https://kubernetes.io/docs/concepts/cluster-administration/networking/`.

We will be deploying a CNI plugin called `amazon-vpc-cni-k8s` that integrates Kubernetes with the native networking capabilities of the AWS VPC network. This plugin works by attaching secondary private IP addresses to the elastic network interfaces of the EC2 instances that form the nodes of our cluster, and then assigning them to pods as they are scheduled by Kubernetes to go into each node. Traffic is then routed directly to the correct node by the AWS VPC network fabric.

Deploying this plugin is a similar process to submitting any other manifest to the Kubernetes API with `kubectl`, as shown in the following command:

```
$ kubectl apply -f
https://raw.githubusercontent.com/aws/amazon-vpc-cni-k8s/master/config/v1.3
/aws-k8s-cni.yaml
daemonset "aws-node" created
```

You can monitor the networking plugin that is being installed and started by running the following:

```
$ kubectl -n kube-system describe pods aws-node
```

We can check that the network has been set up correctly by looking at the node status again, as follows:

```
$ kubectl get nodes
NAME                STATUS    ROLES     AGE      VERSION
ip-172-31-29-230    Ready     master    10m      v1.9.3
```

Launching worker nodes

We are now going to create a new security group for the worker nodes, as follows:

```
$ K8S_NODES_SG_ID=$(aws ec2 create-security-group \
    --group-name k8s-nodes \
    --description "Kubernetes Nodes" \
    --vpc-id $VPC_ID \
    --query GroupId \
    --output text)
```

We will allow access to the worker nodes via the bastion host in order for us to log in for debugging purposes, as follows:

```
$ aws ec2 authorize-security-group-ingress \
    --group-id $K8S_NODES_SG_ID \
    --protocol tcp \
    --port 22 \
    --source-group $BASTION_SG_ID
```

We want to allow the kubelet and other processes running on the worker nodes to be able to connect to the API server on the master node. We do this using the following command:

```
$ aws ec2 authorize-security-group-ingress \
    --group-id $K8S_MASTER_SG_ID \
    --protocol tcp \
    --port 6443 \
    --source-group $K8S_NODES_SG_ID
```

Since the kube-dns add-on may run on the master node, let's allow this traffic from the nodes security group, as follows:

```
$ aws ec2 authorize-security-group-ingress \
    --group-id $K8S_MASTER_SG_ID \
    --protocol all \
    --port 53 \
    --source-group $K8S_NODES_SG_ID
```

We also need the master node to be able to connect to the APIs that are exposed by the kubelet in order to stream logs and other metrics. We enable this by entering the following command:

```
$ aws ec2 authorize-security-group-ingress \
    --group-id $K8S_NODES_SG_ID \
    --protocol tcp \
    --port 10250 \
    --source-group $K8S_MASTER_SG_ID
$ aws ec2 authorize-security-group-ingress \
    --group-id $K8S_NODES_SG_ID \
    --protocol tcp \
    --port 10255 \
    --source-group $K8S_MASTER_SG_ID
```

Finally, we need to allow any pod on any node to be able to connect to any other pod. We do this using the following command:

```
$ aws ec2 authorize-security-group-ingress \
    --group-id $K8S_NODES_SG_ID \
    --protocol all \
    --port -1 \
    --source-group $K8S_NODES_SG_ID
```

In order to have the worker node(s) register themselves with the master when they start up, we will create a user-data script.

This script is run on the first occasion that the node is started. It makes some configuration changes, then runs `kubeadm join`, as shown in the following command. You should have made a note of the `kubeadm join` command when we initialized the master.

```
user-data.sh
#!/bin/bash
set -exuo pipefail
hostnamectl set-hostname $(curl
http://169.254.169.254/latest/meta-data/hostname)
cat << EOF $ /etc/systemd/system/kubelet.service.d/20-aws.conf
[Service]
Environment="KUBELET_EXTRA_ARGS=--cloud-provider=aws --node-ip=$(curl
http://169.254.169.254/latest/meta-data/local-ipv4)    --node-labels=node-
role.kubernetes.io/node="
EOF
systemctl daemon-reload
systemctl restart kubelet
kubeadm join \
  --token fddaf9.1f07b60a8268aac0 \
  --discovery-token-ca-cert-hash
sha256:872757bce0df91c2b046b0d8bb5d930bc1ecfa245b14c25ad8a52746cb8b8e8b \
10.0.0.10:6443
```

First, we create a launch configuration using the following command. This is like a template of the configuration that the autoscaling group will use to launch our worker nodes. Many of the arguments are similar to those that we would have passed to the EC2 run-instances command:

```
$ aws autoscaling create-launch-configuration \
    --launch-configuration-name k8s-node-1.10.3-t2-medium-001 \
    --image-id $K8S_AMI_ID \
    --key-name
  eds_laptop \
    --security-groups $K8S_NODES_SG_ID \
    --user-data file://user-data.sh \
    --instance-type t2.medium \
    --iam-instance-profile K8sNode \
    --no-associate-public-ip-address
```

Once we have created the launch configuration, we can create an autoscaling group, as follows:

```
> aws autoscaling create-auto-scaling-group \
    --auto-scaling-group-name hopper-t2-medium-nodes \
    --launch-configuration-name k8s-node-1.10.3-t2-medium-001 \
    --min-size 1 \
    --max-size 1 \
```

```
    --vpc-zone-identifier $PRIVATE_SUBNET_ID \
    --tags Key=Name,Value=hopper-k8s-node \
      Key=kubernetes.io/cluster/hopper,Value=owned \
      Key=k8s.io/cluster-autoscaler/enabled,Value=1
```

You will need to wait a few moments for the autoscaling group to launch the node, and for `kubeadm` to register it with the master, as follows.

```
> kubectl get nodes --watch
NAME              STATUS    AGE      VERSION
ip-10-0-0-10      Ready     37m      v1.10.3
ip-10-0-2-135     Ready     53s      v1.10.3
```

 If your node starts but doesn't join the cluster after a few minutes, try logging into the node and looking at the `cloud-init` log file. The end of this log will include the output from your script.

```
> cat /var/log/cloud-init-output.log
```

Demo time

Congratulations, if you have made it this far through the chapter! You should by now have a fully functional Kubernetes cluster that you can use to experiment with and explore Kubernetes more fully.

Let's demonstrate that the cluster we have built is working by deploying an application to our cluster, as follows:

```
kubectl apply -f
https://raw.githubusercontent.com/PacktPublishing/Kubernetes-on-AWS/master/
chapter03/demo.yaml
```

This manifest deploys a simple web application and a service to expose the application to the internet using a load balancer. We can view the public DNS name of the load balancer by using the `kubectl get service` command, as follows:

```
> kubectl get svc demo -o wide
```

Once you have the public address of the load balancer, you might need to wait for a few moments before the address starts to resolve. Visit the address in your browser; you should see a screen like the following:

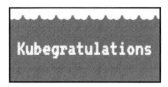

Summary

By now, you should have a fully functional Kubernetes cluster that you can use to experiment with and explore Kubernetes more fully. Your cluster is correctly configured to take advantage of the many integrations that Kubernetes has with AWS.

While there are many tools that can automate and assist you in the task of building and managing a Kubernetes cluster on AWS, hopefully by learning how to approach the task from scratch, you will have a better understanding of the networking and computing resources needed to support a Kubernetes cluster.

In Part 3, we will build on the knowledge from this chapter and discuss the additional components that you will need to add to a cluster to make it suitable for hosting production services. The cluster we have just built is a fully functional installation of Kubernetes. Read on as we look at the tools and techniques required to successfully operate production services on Kubernetes:

- We will look at the tools and procedures you can adopt to manage deploying and updating your services effectively using Kubernetes
- We will look at the strategies and tools you can adopt to secure your cluster and the applications running on it
- We will look at the tools typically used with Kubernetes for monitoring and log management
- We will look at the best ways to architect your applications and your clusters in order to meet availability targets

4

Managing Change in Your Applications

In `Chapter 2`, *Start Your Engines*, we took a first look at running an application on Kubernetes using deployments. In this chapter, we are going to go into depth with tools that Kubernetes provides to manage the pods that we run on your cluster.

- We will learn how to ensure that batch tasks are successfully completed by using the `Job` resource
- We will learn how to run jobs at scheduled intervals with the `CronJob` resource
- Finally, we will learn how to use deployments to keep long-running applications running indefinitely, and to update them or their configuration when changes need to be made

We will look at how we can launch pods in different ways with Kubernetes, depending on the workloads we are running.

You will learn a lot more about how to use the deployment resource to control the way Kubernetes rolls out changes to long-running applications. You will discover the ways you can use Kubernetes to perform common deploy patterns, such as blue-green and canary deployments.

By design, pods are not intended to be durable in any way. As we have discussed previously, there is a whole raft of conditions that can cause the life of a pod to be terminated. They include:

- **The failure of an underlying node**: Perhaps caused by some unexpected event, such as a hardware failure. Or perhaps by design; for example in a cluster utilizing spot priced instances nodes can be terminated without warning if demand for instances increases.

- **Pod evictions initiated by the scheduler**: The scheduler can initiate pod evictions when it needs to in order to optimize the usage of resources on the cluster. This could be because some processes have a higher priority than others, or just to optimize bin packing on the cluster.
- Pods manually removed by the user.
- Pods removed due to planned maintenance; for example, by using the `kubectl drain` command.
- The node is no longer visible to the cluster due to a network partition.
- Pods removed from the node in preparation of a scaling down action.

So, if the design of Kubernetes expects pods to ephemeral, how can we deploy reliable applications? Surely, we need some way to run our programs without fail? Thankfully, this is not exactly the case. The important part of this design is that it accurately models the wide range of issues that can occur in the system due to the underlying hardware and software, and as a result of management processes. Rather than trying to make the primitive building block (the pod) resilient to failures itself, Kubernetes provides a number of controllers that we, as users, can interact with directly to build resilient services. These controllers handle creating replacements for pods that have been lost for any number of reasons.

These controllers fall into four groups, and our choice really depends on the type of workload we want to run:

- For processes that we expect to end, such as batch jobs or other finite processes, Kubernetes provides the job abstraction. Jobs ensure that a pod runs to completion at least once.
- For pods that we expect to be long-running, such as a web server or a background processing worker, Kubernetes provides deployments and the lower level ReplicationController or ReplicaSet.
- For pods that we want to run on all machines (or a subset of them), Kubernetes provides DaemonSet. DaemonSet are typically used to provide machine-specific services that form part of your platform, such as log management or monitoring agents, and commonly to deploy per node components of an overlay network.
- For groups of pods where each pod requires a stable identity or to access persistent storage, Kubernetes provides `StatefulSets`. (We will cover `StatefulSets` in Chapter 9, *Storing State*.)

If you think back to what we learned about the architecture of Kubernetes in `Chapter 1`, *Google's Infrastructure for the Rest of Us*, it is important to remember that the controller manager (the Kubernetes micro service that runs all these controllers) is a separate and distinct process from the scheduler. The core lower-level parts of Kubernetes, such as the scheduler and the kubelet, only know about pods, whereas the higher-level controllers don't need to understand any of the details of actually scheduling and running pods on nodes. They just make a request to the API server for a pod to be created and the lower-level machinery ensures that they are scheduled and run correctly.

In this chapter, we are going to walk through the important features and configuration options that jobs, deployments, and DaemonSet provide us. By working through some examples, you will start to get a feel for when to use each resource to deploy your applications. You should take your time to understand what each controller is doing and why you would want to use it.

Deploying software to a distributed environment can be a little bit unusual at first, because a lot of assumptions you might have made about the way that your software runs when deploying it to a single machine might not work in a distributed system.

Kubernetes does a great job of making it possible to deploy most software without any modifications at all. I like to think that Kubernetes lets us trade a little simplicity for a lot of reliability.

Running pods directly

Kubernetes doesn't really intend for users to directly submit and launch pods on the cluster. As we discussed previously, pods are designed to be ephemeral, so are not suitable for running workloads where we want to ensure that execution has completed or where we want to ensure that a process remains up and running.

Here, we will start from first principles, launching pods, before moving on to use a controller to help us manage them. Bear in mind that this is a learning exercise; you shouldn't submit pods in this way if you need them to run reliably:

```
pod.yaml
apiVersion: v1
kind: Pod
metadata:
  name: hello-loop
spec:
  containers:
  - name: loop
    image: alpine
```

```
command: ["/bin/sh"]
args:
- -c
- while true; do echo "hello world"; sleep 2s; done
```

This pod launches an infinite loop that prints `hello world` every 2 seconds. Start by submitting the pod to the cluster with `kubectl`:

```
$ kubectl create -f pod.yaml
pod "hello-loop" created
```

It might take a few moments for the pod be created while the container runtime downloads the image. While this is happening, you could check on the status of the pod by running `kubectl describe pod/hello-loop` or by using the dashboard.

The fact that Kubernetes makes it possible to control even the lowest-level abstractions, such as pods, through the API makes it easy to extend Kubernetes with additional functionality using or building add-on tools that can be just as powerful as the built-in controllers.

Once the pod is up and running, you can follow the output with `kubectl logs -f hello-loop` and you should see `hello world` output every 2 seconds.

`kubectl logs` allows us to display logs from pods that have run on the cluster. If you know the name of the pod you want logs from, you can just pass the name as an argument. But if you are using a controller to launch a pod, you can use the name of a job or deployment in place of the pod name just by prefixing the name with the resource type.

If you have a label selector for the pod or pods you are interested in, they can be passed with the `-l` flag. With the `-c` flag, you can target a specific named container in a pod with more than one container; if the pod only has one container, this can be omitted.

Try running `kubectl`. It helps logs to discover some more of the options you can use to view just the logs you are interested in, including limiting them to a particular time period.

Jobs

The simplest use case for a job is to launch a single pod and ensure that it successfully runs to completion.

In our next example, we are going to use the Ruby programming language to compute and print out the first 100 Fibonacci numbers:

```
fib.yaml
apiVersion: batch/v1
kind: Job
metadata:
  name: fib
spec:
  template:
    metadata:
      name: fib
    spec:
      containers:
      - name: fib
        image: ruby:alpine
        command: ["ruby"]
        args:
        - -e
        - |
          a,b = 0,1
          100.times { puts b = (a = a+b) - b }
      restartPolicy: Never
```

Notice that the contents of `spec` and `template` are very similar to the specification we used to launch a pod directly. When we define a pod template for use in a job, we need to choose a `restartPolicy` of `Never` or `OnFailure`.

The reason for this is that the end goal of a job is to run the pod until it exits successfully. If the underlying pod is restarted when it exits successfully, the pod would continue to be restarted and the job would never complete.

Save the definition to a file and then submit it to the cluster using `kubectl create`:

```
$ kubectl create -f fib.yaml
job "fib" created
```

Once you have submitted a job to Kubernetes, you can check on its status with the `kubectl describe` command. It might take a little while for the Docker image to download and Kubernetes to launch the pod. Once the pod is running, you should see first 1 `Running` and then 1 `Succeeded` in the `Pods Statues` field:

```
$ kubectl describe jobs/fib
Name: fib
Namespace: default
Selector: controller-uid=278fa785-9b86-11e7-b25b-080027e071f1
Labels: controller-uid=278fa785-9b86-11e7-b25b-080027e071f1
  job-name=fib
Annotations: <none>
Parallelism: 1
Completions: 1
Start Time: Sun, 17 Sep 2017 09:56:54 +0100
Pods Statuses: 0 Running / 1 Succeeded / 0 Failed
```

When waiting for Kubernetes to take some action, repeatedly running `kubectl` to find out what is happening can get tedious. I like to use the `watch` command in conjunction with `kubectl`. To watch Kubernetes launch this job, I could run:

```
$ watch kubectl describe jobs/fib
```

Most Linux distributions will include the watch command by default, or make it simple to install with a package manager. If you are on macOS, it's very simple to install with Homebrew:

```
$ brew install watch
```

We can use `kubectl logs` to view the output from our job. Notice how we don't need to know the name of the underlying pod(s); we can just refer to the job by name:

```
$ kubectl logs job/fib
...
83621143489848422977
135301852344706746049
218922995834555169026
```

We can also look at the underlying pod that was created by this job with `kubectl get` by using the `job-name` label that Kubernetes adds to the pods for us:

```
$ kubectl get pods -l job-name=fib --show-all
NAME READY STATUS RESTARTS AGE
fib-dg4zh 0/1 Completed 0 1m
```

> The `--show-all` flag means that all pods are shown (even those that no longer have a running status).

Notice how Kubernetes created a unique name for our pod based on the job name. This is important because if the first pod to have been created failed in some way, Kubernetes would need to launch another pod based on the same pod specification.

One of the key advantages jobs have over launching a pod directly is that a job is able to handle not only errors caused by the underlying infrastructure that might cause a pod to be lost before it has completed, but also errors that occur at runtime.

To illustrate how this works, this job simulates a process that (mostly) fails with a non-zero exit status, but sometimes exits with a (successful) zero exit status. This Ruby program chooses a random integer from 0 to 10 and exits with it. So, on average, Kubernetes will have to run the pod 10 times before it exits successfully:

```
luck.yaml
apiVersion: batch/v1
kind: Job
metadata:
  name: luck
spec:
  template:
    metadata:
      name: luck
    spec:
      containers:
      - name: luck
        image: ruby:alpine
        command: ["ruby"]
        args: ["-e", "exit rand(10)"]
      restartPolicy: Never
```

As before, submit the job to your cluster with `kubectl`:

```
$ kubectl create -f luck.yaml
job "luck" created
```

Unless you are very lucky, when you inspect the job, you should see that Kubernetes has to launch a number of pods before one exited with 0 status:

	Name ⇕	Node	Status ⇕	Restarts	Age ⇕		
!	luck-43ghc	minikube	Terminated: Error	0	6 seconds		
✓	luck-hmrc9	minikube	Terminated: Completed	0	5 seconds		
!	luck-klr3n	minikube	Terminated: Error	0	8 seconds		
!	luck-zf47t	minikube	Terminated: Error	0	7 seconds		

Inspecting the pods launched by the luck job using the Kubernetes dashboard

In this example, the pod spec has a `restartPolicy` of `Never`. This means that when the pod exits with a non-zero exit status, the pod is marked as terminated and the job controller launches another pod. It is also possible to run jobs with a `restartPolicy` of `OnFailure`.

Try editing `luck.yaml` to make this change. Remove the first version of the `luck` job and submit your new version:

```
$ kubectl delete jobs/luck
job "luck" deleted
$ kubectl create -f luck.yaml
job "luck" created
```

This time, you should notice that instead of quickly launching new pods until one exits successfully, Kubernetes restarts one pod until it is successful. You will notice that this takes quite a bit longer, because when Kubernetes restarts a pod locally with an exponential back-off, this behavior is useful if a failure was caused by an underlying resource that is overloaded or unavailable. You might notice the pod in a status of `CrashLoopBackoff` while Kubernetes is waiting to restart the pod:

```
$ kubectl get pods -l job-name=luck -a
NAME READY STATUS RESTARTS AGE
luck-0kptd 0/1 Completed 5 3m
```

Allowing the job controller to recreate a new pod each time it terminates in error ensures that the new pod is run in a new pristine environment and causes the job resource to retain a record of each execution attempt. For this reason, it is usually best not to utilize a pod restart policy in conjunction with a job, unless you have to deal with pods that regularly fail or if you want to retain the execution environment between attempts.

CronJob

Now you have learned how to run one-off or batch tasks with jobs, it is simple to extend the concept in order to run scheduled jobs. In Kubernetes, a `CronJob` is a controller that creates new jobs from a template on a given schedule.

Let's begin with a simple example. The following example will launch a job every minute. This job will output the current date and time and then exit:

```
fun-with-cron.yaml
apiVersion: batch/v1beta1
kind: CronJob
metadata:
  name: fun-with-cron
spec:
  schedule: "* * * * *"
  jobTemplate:
    spec:
      template:
        metadata:
          labels:
            cronjob: fun-with-cron
        spec:
          restartPolicy: OnFailure
          containers:
          - name: how-soon-is-now
            image: alpine:3.6
            command: ["/bin/date"]
```

Push the CronJob to Kubernetes with `kubectl`:

```
$ kubectl apply -f fun-with-cron.yaml
```

After some time (less than a minute), you should see the first job created:

```
$ kubectl get jobs
NAME DESIRED SUCCESSFUL AGE
fun-with-cron-1533475680 1 1 9s
```

The label we added to the pod template spec allows us to use `kubectl logs` to see the output of all the pods created by the CronJob:

```
$ kubectl logs -l cronjob=fun-with-cron
  Sun Aug 5 13:26:08 UTC 2018
  Sun Aug 5 13:27:08 UTC 2018
  Sun Aug 5 13:28:08 UTC 2018
```

Cron syntax

The syntax of the schedule field follows the standard Cron format, which should be familiar if you have ever set up CronJobs on a Unix-like system. Kubernetes supports standard cron strings with a few common extensions.

A standard cron string consists of five fields that each represent different units of time. Each can be set to an expression representing a particular time, or a wildcard (*) that would match every time. For example, a wildcard in the **Months** column would match every month:

Minutes	Hours	Day of Month	Month	Day of Week

Order of cron fields

The cron format is simplest to understand if it is read from left to right. Here are some examples:

- `0 * * * *`: On the hour, every hour
- `15 * * * *`: 15 minutes past every hour
- `0 0 * * *`: At midnight, every day
- `30 5 1 * *`: 5:30 a.m. on the first day of the month, every month
- `30 17 * * 1`: 15:30 p.m., every Monday

As well as the wildcard, there are a few other characters with special meaning.

Slashes are used to indicate steps:

- `0/15 * * * *`: Every 15 minutes, starting at 0; for example, 12:00, 12:15, 12:30, and so on
- `15/15 * * * *`: Every 15 minutes, starting at 15; for example, 12:15, 12:30, 12:45, 13:15, 13:30, and so on
- `0 0 0/10 * *`: Every 10 days at midnight

Hyphens indicate ranges:

- 0 9-17 * * *: Once an hour during office hours (9 a.m. till 5 p.m.)
- 0 0 1-15/2 * *: Every other day for the first 15 days of every month

Commas indicate lists:

- 0 0 * * 6,0: Midnight on Saturday and Sunday
- 0 9,12,17 * * 1-5: At 9:00 a.m., 12 noon, and 5:00 p.m., Monday to Friday

As an aid to readability, names can be used in the month and day of the week fields:

- 0 0 * * SUN: Midnight on Sunday
- 0 6 * MAR-MAY *: 6 a.m. every day in Spring

If you don't mind when exactly a job is run, you can specify a fixed interval and Kubernetes will create jobs at a fixed interval:

- @every 15m: Every 15 minutes
- @every 1h30m: Every 1-and-a half hours
- @every 12h: Every 12 hours

Bear in mind that the interval doesn't take the time that the job takes to run into account; it just ensures that the time that each job is scheduled is separated by the given interval.

Finally, there are several predefined schedules that can be used as a shortcut in place of a cron string:

Shortcut	Equivalent cron	
@hourly	0 0 * * * *	Every hour, on the hour
@daily	0 0 0 * * *	Every day at midnight
@weekly	0 0 0 * * 0	Every week midnight on Sunday
@monthly	0 0 0 1 * *	Monthly, at midnight on the 1st
@yearly	0 0 0 1 1 *	Midnight, every New Year's Eve

Concurrency policy

Kubernetes CronJob, in contrast to the traditional CronJob, allows us to decide what happens when a job overruns and we reach the scheduled time while the previous job is still running. We can control this behavior by setting the `spec.concurrencyPolicy` field on the CronJob. There are three possible policies that we can choose:

- By default, if the field is unset then we get the `Allow` policy. This behaves just like a traditional CronJob and allows multiple instances of a job to run at the same time. If you stick with this, you should be sure that your jobs indeed get completed at some point, or your cluster could end up overwhelmed with many jobs running at the same time.
- The `Forbid` policy prevents any new jobs from starting while an existing job is still running. This means that if a job overruns, Kubernetes will skip the next run. This is a good choice if having two or more instances of a job running could cause conflicts or use up shared resources. Your job, of course, does need to be able to account for missing runs in this case.
- Finally, the `Replace` policy also prevents more than one job from running at once, but rather than skipping a run, it first kills the existing job and then launches a new job.

History limits

By default, when you use a CronJob, the jobs that it creates will stick around, so you can check on what happened to a particular run of a job for debugging or reporting. You might, however, find that the number of jobs in the successful or failed state starts to pile up quite quickly when using CronJob. This is simple to manage with the `spec.successfulJobsHistoryLimit` and `spec.failedJobsHistoryLimit` fields. Once the successful, or failed jobs reach the number specified in the limit, the oldest job is deleted each time a new job is created. If you set a limit to 0, the jobs are removed as soon as they complete.

Managing long running processes with deployments

Updating batch processes, such as jobs and CronJobs, is relatively easy. Since they have a limited lifetime, the simplest strategy of updating code or configurations is just to update the resources in question before they are used again.

Long-running processes are a little harder to deal with, and even harder to manage if you are exposing a service to the network. Kubernetes provides us with the deployment resource to make deploying and, more importantly, updating long-running processes simpler.

In `Chapter 2`, *Start Your Engines*, we took a first look at the deployment resource, both creating deployments with `kubectl run` and by defining a deployment object in a YAML file. In this chapter, we will recap the process that the deployment controller uses to roll out changes, and then look in to some of the more advanced options for controlling exactly how new versions of the pods are made available. We will cover how we can use deployments in conjunction with services to make changes to services provided on the network without downtime.

Much like CronJob is a controller for jobs, a deployment is a controller for ReplicaSets. A ReplicaSet makes sure that the required number of pods for a particular configuration is up and running. In order to manage a change to this configuration, the deployment controller creates a new ReplicaSet with the new configuration, and then scales the old ReplicaSet down and the new one up, according to a particular strategy. A deployment will maintain a reference to the old ReplicaSet even after the deployment of the new configuration is complete. This allows the deployment to also orchestrate a rollback to a previous version if required.

Let's begin with an example application that will allow you to quickly understand how the different options offered by deployments allow you to manipulate the behavior of your application during an update to your code or configuration.

We will be deploying an application that I created to make it simple to illustrate deploying new versions of software with Kubernetes. It is a simple Ruby web application in a Docker repository that has many version tags. Each version displays a unique name and color scheme when the homepage is opened in a browser.

When we deploy a long-running process to Kubernetes, we can roll out access to the application in a controlled manner using labels.

The simplest strategy to implement is to use a single deployment to roll out changes to a new version of your applications.

To implement this, we need to start by creating a service with a label selector that will match every version of the application that we might deploy now, or in the future:

```
service.yaml
apiVersion: v1
kind: Service
metadata:
```

```
    name: ver
spec:
  selector:
    app: ver
  ports:
  - protocol: TCP
    port: 80
    targetPort: http
```

In this case, we have achieved this by matching any pod that has a label matching the `selector` as `app: ver`.

When running a more complicated application that has several different processes managed by multiple deployments, your labels and selectors will need to be more complicated. A common pattern is to distinguish between the component parts of an application with a `component` label.

 It makes sense to submit the service definition before you start any pods. This is because the scheduler will, if possible, try to spread the pods used by a particular service across multiple nodes for greater reliability.

Submit the service definition to your cluster using `kubectl apply -f service.yaml`.

Once the service has been submitted to the cluster, we can prepare the initial deployment:

```
deployment.yaml
apiVersion: apps/v1
kind: Deployment
metadata:
  name: versions
  labels:
    app: ver
spec:
  replicas: 2
  selector:
    matchLabels:
      app: ver
  template:
    metadata:
      labels:
        app: ver
        version: 0.0.1
    spec:
      containers:
      - name: version-server
        image: errm/versions:0.0.1
```

```
        ports:
        - name: http
          containerPort: 3000
```

To access the running service, the simplest way is to use `kubectl` to open a proxy to the Kubernetes API running on your cluster:

```
$ kubectl proxy
Starting to serve on 127.0.0.1:8001
```

Once you have done, you should be able to view the app using your browser at `http://localhost:8001/api/v1/namespaces/default/services/ver/proxy`.

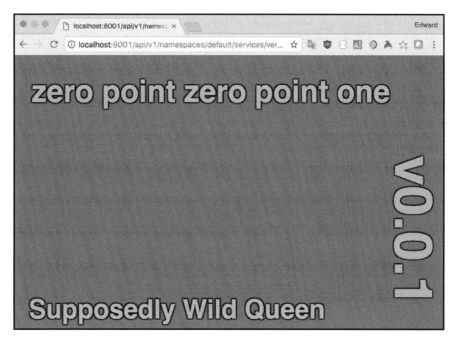

Version 0.0.1 running in our cluster

There are a number of ways that we can now make changes to our deployment.

kubectl patch

To upgrade to version 0.0.2, we will execute the following command:

```
$ kubectl patch deployment/versions -p '
{"spec":{"template":{"spec":{"containers":[{"name":"version-server",
```

```
"image":"errm/versions:0.0.2"}] }}}}'
```

Because containers is a list, we need to specify the merge key `name` for Kubernetes to understand which container we want to update the image field on.

With the `patch` command, Kubernetes performs a merge, merging the JSON provided with the current definition of the `deployment/versions` object.

Go ahead and reload the app in your browser, and then you should notice (after a few seconds) that the new version of the app becomes available.

kubectl edit

To upgrade to version 0.0.3, we are going to use the `kubectl edit` command:

```
kubectl edit deployment/versions
```

`kubectl edit` uses your system's *standard* editor to edit Kubernetes resources. This is often vi, vim, or even ed, but if you have another text editor you prefer you should set up the `EDITOR` environment variable to point at your preferred choice.

This should open your editor, so you can make changes to the deployment. Once this has happened, edit the image field to use version 0.0.3 and save the file.

You might notice that there are more fields in the object opened in your editor than the original file you submitted to Kubernetes. This is because Kubernetes is storing metadata about the current status of the deployment in this object.

kubectl apply

To update to version 0.0.4, we are going to use the `apply` command. This allows us to submit the full resource to Kubernetes just like when we made the initial deployment.

Start by editing your deployment YAML file, and then update the image field to use version 0.0.4. Save the file and then use `kubectl` to submit it to Kubernetes:

```
$ kubectl apply -f deployment.yaml
```

> If you use `kubectl apply` for a resource that doesn't yet exist, it will be created for you. This can be useful if you are using it in a scripted deployment.

The advantage of using `kubectl apply` rather than edit or patch is that you can keep a file checked into version control to represent the state of your cluster.

Kubernetes dashboard

The Kubernetes dashboard includes a tree-based editor that allows you to edit resources right in the browser. On Minikube, you can run the Minikube dashboard to open the dashboard in your browser. You can then choose your deployment and click on the edit button at the top of the page:

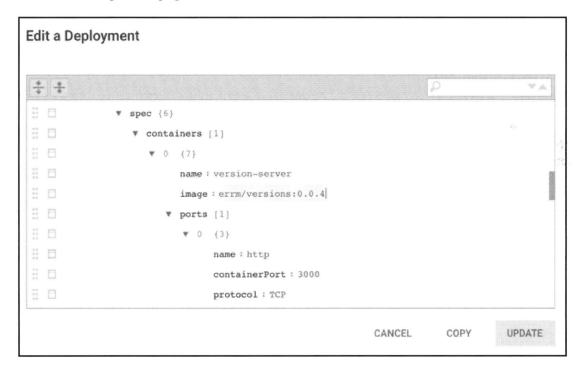

You should be able to find the container image field by scrolling or with the search function. It is simple to click on a value to edit it and then press **UPDATE**.

While you are learning about Kubernetes and experimenting with different configurations, the method you use for updating your configuration should be your own personal preference. Using the Kubernetes dashboard or tools such as `kubectl edit` are great for learning and debugging. But when you move forward to a production environment, you will want to move toward checking your configuration into version control, or using a tool such as Helm (which we will discuss in `Chapter 5`, *Managing Complex Applications with Helm*).

Greater control of your deployments

By now we have covered a number of ways that we can update resources in Kubernetes. As we have observed, when we update a deployment in Kubernetes, eventually the pods in the cluster are updated to reflect the new configuration.

Kubernetes achieves this by managing ReplicaSets behind the scenes.

The ReplicaSet is purely concerned with managing a set of pods to ensure that the desired number of replicas are running on the cluster. During an update, the pod spec of the existing ReplicaSet is never changed. The deployment controller creates a new ReplicaSet with the new pod configuration. The roll-out of this new configuration is orchestrated by altering the desired number of replicas for each ReplicaSet.

This separation of concerns is typical of the way that resources are designed in Kubernetes. More complex behavior is achieved by orchestrating simpler objects, whose controllers implement simpler behaviors.

This design also makes it quite simple for us (the cluster operator) to decide exactly what behavior we want when we update our configuration. The `spec.stratergy` field is used to configure the behavior that is used when changes are rolled out.

The `.spec.strategy.type` field defines the strategy that is used to replace the old pods with new ones. Currently, there are two strategies: `Recreate` and `RollingUpdate`. `RollingUpdate` is the default strategy, so normally you won't need to specify it in your configuration.

RollingUpdate deployment

`.spec.strategy.type=RollingUpdate is the default strategy`. This is the strategy that we have been using in our examples so far.

You would specifically choose a rolling update whenever you want to update without interruption to service. Conversely, your application has to work correctly when multiple versions are running at the same time if you use this strategy.

When using the `RollingUpdate` strategy, there are two settings that allow us to specify how quickly the new ReplicaSet is scaled up and how quickly the old ReplicaSet is scaled down:

- `.spec.strategy.rollingUpdate.maxUnavailable`: It specifies the number of pods that can be unavailable (out of the desired total) during the deployment process
- `.spec.strategy.rollingUpdate.maxSurge`: It specifies the number of pods that can be created over and above the desired total during the deployment process

These settings accept either absolute values, such as 1 or 0, or a percentage of the total desired number of pods on the deployment. A percentage value is useful if you intend for this configuration to be reusable across different deployments that are scaled to different levels, or if you intend to control the desired number of pods with an auto-scaling mechanism.

By setting `maxUnavailable` to 0, Kubernetes will wait till replacement pod(s) have been scheduled and are running before killing any pods managed by the old ReplicationSet. If `maxUnavailable` is used in this way, then during the deployment process, Kubernetes will run more than the desired number of pods so `maxSurge` cannot be 0, and you must have the required resources (in a cluster, and for backing services) to support temporarily running the extra instances during the deployment phase.

Once Kubernetes has launched all the instances, it it must wait until the new pods are in service and in the `Ready` state. This means that if you have set up health checks for your pod, the deployment will pause if these are failing.

If `maxSurge` and/or `maxUnavailable` are set to low values, your deployments will take longer as the deployment will pause and wait for the new pod(s) to become available before moving forward. This can be useful, as it provides you a degree of protection against deploying broken code or configurations.

Setting `maxSurge` to a bigger value will decrease the number of scaling steps the deployment takes to update the application. If, for example, you were to set `maxSurge` to 100% and `maxUnavailable` to 0 then Kubernetes would create all the replacement pods as soon as the deployment starts and kill the existing pods as the new ones enter the Ready state.

Exactly how you want to configure your deployments will depend on the requirements of your application and the resources available to your cluster.

You should bear in mind that setting `maxSurge` to lower values will give you slower deployments that take longer to complete, but may be more resilient to errors, whereas, with higher `maxSurge` values, your deployments will progress faster. But your cluster will need to have enough capacity to support the additional running instances. If your application accesses other services, you should also be aware of the additional load that might be placed on them. For example, databases can be configured to have a limit to the number of connections that they accept.

Recreate deployment

`.spec.strategy.type=Recreate` takes a much simpler approach to rolling out changes to your application. First, all the pods with the previous configuration are terminated by scaling down the active ReplicaSet, and then a new ReplicaSet is created that starts replacement pods.

This strategy is particularly appropriate when you don't mind short periods of downtime. For example, with background processing, when workers or other tasks don't need to provide services that are accessed over the network. The advantages in these use cases are twofold. Firstly, you don't have to worry about any incompatibilities caused by two versions of your code running at the same time. Secondly, of course, with this strategy the process of updating your pods uses no more resources that your application would normally need.

DaemonSet

If you want a single instance of a particular pod to be running on every node of your cluster (or a subset of your nodes), then you need to use a DaemonSet. When you schedule a DaemonSet to your cluster, an instance of your pod will be scheduled to every node, and when you add new nodes, the pod is scheduled there too. DaemonSet are very useful for providing ubiquitous services that need to be available everywhere on your cluster. You might use DaemonSet to provide services such as:

- An agent to ingest and ship logs, such as Fluentd or Logstash
- A monitoring agent, such as collectd, Prometheus Node Exporter, datadog, NewRelic or SysDig, and so on
- A daemon for a distributed storage system, such as Gluster or Ceph
- Components for an overlay network, such as Calico or Flannel
- Per node components, a virtualization tool, such as OpenStack

Before Kubernetes, these sorts of services would require you to configure an init system, such as `systemd` or SysVnit, on every server in your infrastructure. When you came to update the service or its configuration, you would have to update that configuration and restart services across all your servers, which is not a problem when you are managing a few servers, but with tens, hundreds, or even thousands of servers, things quickly become much harder to manage.

DaemonSet lets you use exactly the same configuration and containerization we have been applying to the applications that run on your infrastructure to manage the infrastructure itself.

Let's look at a simple example to understand how we can create a DaemonSet for a useful purpose. We will be deploying the Prometheus Node Exporter. The purpose of this application is to expose an HTTP endpoint that includes metrics about the Linux system it is running on.

 If you decide to monitor your cluster, PrometheusNode Exporter is a very useful tool. If you do decide to run it in your own cluster, I would recommend that you look at the extensive documentation available on the GitHub page at `https://github.com/prometheus/node_exporter`.

This manifest causes the pod specified in the template section to be scheduled to every node in your cluster:

```
node-exporter.yaml
apiVersion: apps/v1
kind: DaemonSet
metadata:
  labels:
    app: node-exporter
  name: node-exporter
spec:
  selector:
    matchLabels:
      app: node-exporter
  template:
    metadata:
      labels:
        app: node-exporter
    spec:
      containers:
      - name: node-exporter
        image: quay.io/prometheus/node-exporter:v0.15.2
        args:
        - --path.procfs=/host/proc
        - --path.sysfs=/host/sys
        volumeMounts:
        - mountPath: /host/proc
          name: proc
          readOnly: false
        - mountPath: /host/sys
          name: sys
          readOnly: false
        ports:
        - containerPort: 9100
          hostPort: 9100
      hostNetwork: true
      hostPID: true
      volumes:
      - hostPath:
          path: /proc
        name: proc
      - hostPath:
          path: /sys
        name: sys
```

Once you have prepared the manifest file for the Node Exporter, submit it to Kubernetes by running the `kubectl apply -f node-exporter.yaml` command.

You can check if the DaemonSet controller has scheduled our pod to the nodes in your cluster correctly by running the `kubectl describe ds/node-exporter` command. Assuming that the pod is successfully running, you should be able to make an HTTP request to port `9100` on one of your nodes to see the metrics that it exposes.

> If you are trying this example on Minikube, you can discover the IP address of the (only) node in your cluster by running `minikube ip`. Then you can use a tool such as `curl` to make a request:
>
> **curl 192.168.99.100:9100/metrics**

One of the key advantages to using DaemonSet to manage infrastructure tools and components, rather than relying on static configuration on your nodes to manage them, is that they can be updated just as easily as any other application you are running on your cluster.

By default, DaemonSet have an `updateStrategy` of `RollingUpdate`. This means if you edit the pod template in a DaemonSet, the existing pods currently running on the cluster are killed and replaced one by one.

Let's try using this functionality to upgrade to a newer version of the Prometheus Node Exporter:

```
kubectl set image ds/node-exporter node-exporter=quay.io/prometheus/node-
exporter:v0.16.0
```

You can check on the progress of replacing the old pods with the new version by running: `kubectl rollout status ds/node-exporter` command. Once the update is completed, you should see the following message: `daemon set "node-exporter" successfully rolled out`.

> You might be wondering what other `updateStrategys` are available for DaemonSet. The only other option is `OnDelete`. With this option, when a DaemonSet is updated, no changes are made to the running pods running on the cluster, and it is left up to you to manually delete the running pods before the new version is launched. This mainly exists to provide compatibility with the behavior in previous versions of Kubernetes and is not, in practice, very useful.

It is worth bearing in mind that in order to roll out a new version of a pod with a DaemonSet, there will be a short period between the old pod being killed and the new one being launched, during which the service you are running will be unavailable.

DaemonSet can also be used to run pods on a subset of the nodes in your cluster. This is achieved by labeling the nodes in your cluster and adding a `nodeSelector` to the pod spec of your DaemonSet:

```
    . . .
      spec:
        nodeSelector:
          monitoring: prometheus
        containers:
        - name: node-exporter
    . . .
```

Once you have edited your manifest to add the `nodeSelector`, submit the new configuration to Kubernetes with: `kubectl apply -f node-exporter.yaml`.

You should notice that the running node exporter pods are terminated and removed from your cluster. This is because no nodes in your cluster match the label selector that we added to the DaemonSet. Nodes can be labeled on the fly by using `kubectl`:

```
kubectl label node/<node name> monitoring=prometheus
```

Once a node is correctly labeled, you should notice that the DaemonSet controller schedules a pod to it.

On AWS, nodes are automatically labeled with information including region, availability zone, instance type, and hostname. You might wish to use these labels to deploy services to certain nodes in your cluster, or to provide differently configured versions of tools for different types of node in your cluster.
If you want to add additional labels, you can pass them as arguments to the kubelet using the `--node-labels` flag.

Summary

In this chapter, we have learned how to use Kubernetes to run our applications and, importantly, how to roll out new versions of our applications and their configurations.

We built on our basic knowledge of pods and deployments from the previous chapters:

- Pods are the lowest-level abstraction that Kubernetes provides us
- All the other resources that deal with running containers, such as jobs, ScheduledJobs, deployments, and even DaemonSet, work by creating pods in specific ways.
- Normally, we don't want to create pods directly because if the node a pod is running on stops working, then so will the pod. Using one of the higher-level controllers ensures that a new pod will be created to replace failed pods.
- The higher-level resources, such as deployments and DaemonSet, provide a mechanism to replace one version of a pod with a different one in a controlled way. We learned about the different strategies that are available to do this.

Before you move on to the next chapter, take some time to get a feel for how each of the deployment strategies work by observing how they behave during the deployment process. With a little experience, you will develop an understanding of which options to choose for a given application.

In the next chapter, we are going to look at using a tool that builds upon these concepts to provide even more powerful ways to deploy and update your applications.

5

Managing Complex Applications with Helm

In the previous chapters, you started to learn how to build and deploy the configuration needed to run different applications on your Kubernetes cluster.

Once you move beyond deploying the simplest of applications, you will discover that your applications often have one or more components that work in unison. For example, you might have a web application that displays information from a database that also uses a scheduled job to update that information on a regular basis. In order for this application to function correctly, both of these components need to be deployed and functioning correctly. Furthermore, these two components likely share some configuration, such as credentials for the backend database.

One other problem we might encounter when deploying applications to our Kubernetes cluster is one of reusability. Perhaps we need to run the same tool or application in multiple contexts or environments. For example, many organizations have a staging environment for testing new versions of software.

When maintaining multiple environments, we ideally want the configuration in each environment to match as closely as possible, but of course, some differences in configuration are required. Maintaining multiple copies of Kubernetes manifests for each of your environments can be error prone, and gives you no guarantees that an application that worked in one environment will work in another.

Helm is a popular tool in the Kubernetes ecosystem that solves these problems. It gives us a way of building packages (known as charts) of related Kubernetes objects that can be deployed in a cohesive way to a cluster. It also allows us to parameterize these packages, so they can be reused in different contexts and deployed to the varying environments that the services they provide might be needed in.

Like Kubernetes, development of Helm is overseen by the Cloud Native Computing Foundation. As well as Helm (the package manager), the community maintains a repository of standard charts for a wide range of open source software you can install and run on your cluster. From the Jenkins CI server to MySQL or Prometheus, it's simple to install and run complex deployments involving many underlying Kubernetes resources with Helm.

In this chapter, you will learn:

- How to install the `helm` command-line tool
- How to install Helm's in-cluster component, Tiller
- How you can deploy a service to your cluster using a community-maintained chart
- About the syntax you will need to know when creating charts
- How to host your own chart repository in order to share your charts within your organization, or more widely
- Strategies for integrating Helm charts into your own deployment processes

Installing Helm

If you have already set up your own Kubernetes cluster and have correctly configured `kubectl` on your machine, then it is simple to install Helm.

macOS

On macOS, the simplest way to install the Helm client is with Homebrew:

```
$ brew install kubernetes-helm
```

Linux and Windows

Every release of Helm includes prebuilt binaries for Linux, Windows, and macOS. Visit `https://github.com/kubernetes/helm/releases` to download the version you need for your platform.

To install the client, simply unpack and copy the binary onto your path.

For example, on a Linux machine you might do the following:

```
$ tar -zxvf helm-v2.7.2-linux-amd64.tar.gz
$ mv linux-amd64/helm /usr/local/bin/helm
```

Installing Tiller

Once you have the Helm CLI tool installed on your machine, you can go about installing Helm's server-side component, Tiller.

Helm uses the same configuration as `kubectl`, so start by checking which context you will be installing Tiller onto:

```
$ kubectl config current-context
minikube
```

Here, we will be installing Tiller into the cluster referenced by the Minikube context. In this case, this is exactly what we want. If your `kubectl` is not currently pointing to another cluster, you can quickly switch to the context you want to use like this:

```
$ kubectl config use-context minikube
```

If you are still not sure that you are using the correct context, take a quick look at the full config and check that the cluster server field is correct:

```
$ kubectl config view --minify=true
```

The `minify` flag removes any config not referenced by the current context. Once you are happy that the cluster that `kubectl` is connecting to is the correct one, we can set up Helm's local environment and install Tiller on to your cluster:

```
$ helm init
$HELM_HOME has been configured at /Users/edwardrobinson/.helm.
Tiller (the Helm server-side component) has been installed into your
Kubernetes Cluster.
Happy Helming!
```

We can use `kubectl` to check that Tiller is indeed running on our cluster:

```
$ kubectl -n kube-system get deploy -l app=helm
NAME            DESIRED    CURRENT    UP-TO-DATE    AVAILABLE    AGE
tiller-deploy   1          1          1             1            3m
```

Once we have verified that Tiller is correctly running on the cluster, let's use the `version` command. This will validate that we are able to connect correctly to the API of the Tiller server and return the version number of both the CLI and the Tiller server:

```
$ helm version
Client: &version.Version{SemVer:"v2.7.2",
GitCommit:"8478fb4fc723885b155c924d1c8c410b7a9444e6", GitTreeState:"clean"}
Server: &version.Version{SemVer:"v2.7.2",
GitCommit:"8478fb4fc723885b155c924d1c8c410b7a9444e6", GitTreeState:"clean"}
```

Installing a chart

Let's start by installing an application by using one of the charts provided by the community.

 You can discover applications that the community has produced Helm charts for at `https://hub.kubeapps.com/`. As well as making it simple to deploy a wide range of applications to your Kubernetes cluster, it's a great resource for learning some of the best practices the community uses when packaging applications for Helm.

Helm charts can be stored in a repository, so it is simple to install them by name. By default, Helm is already configured to use one remote repository called **Stable**.

This makes it simple for us to try out some commonly used applications as soon as Helm is installed.

Before you install a chart, you will need to know three things:

- The name of the chart you want to install
- The name you will give to this release (If you omit this, Helm will create a random name for this release)
- The namespace on the cluster you want to install the chart into (If you omit this, Helm will use the default namespace)

Helm calls each distinct installation of a particular chart a release. Each release has a unique name that is used if you later want to update, upgrade, or even remove a release from your cluster. Being able to install multiple instances of a chart onto a single cluster makes Helm a little bit different from how we think about traditional package managers that are tied to a single machine, and typically only allow one installation of a particular package at once. But once you have got used to the terminology, it is very simple to understand:

- A **chart** is the package that contains all the information about *how* to install a particular application or tool to the cluster. You can think of it as a template that can be reused to create many different instances or releases of the packaged application or tool.
- A **release** is a named installation of a chart to a particular cluster. By referring to a release by name, Helm can make upgrades to a particular release, updating the version of the installed tool, or making configuration changes.
- A **repository** is an HTTP server storing charts along with an index file. When configured with the location of a repository, the Helm client can install a chart from that repository by downloading it and then making a new release.

Before you can install a chart onto your cluster, you need to make sure that Helm knows about the repository that you want to use. You can list the repositories that are currently in use by running the `helm repo list` command:

```
$ helm repo list
NAME    URL
stable  https://kubernetes-charts.storage.googleapis.com
local   http://127.0.0.1:8879/charts
```

By default, Helm is configured with a repository named stable pointing at the community chart repository and local repository that points at a local address for testing your own local repository. (You need to be running `helm serve` for this.)

Adding a Helm repository to this list is simple with the `helm repo add` command. You can add my Helm repository that contains some example applications related to this book by running the following command:

```
$ helm repo add errm https://charts.errm.co.uk
"errm" has been added to your repositories
```

In order to pull the latest chart information from the configured repositories, you can run the following command:

```
$ helm repo update
Hang tight while we grab the latest from your chart repositories...
...Skip local chart repository
...Successfully got an update from the "errm" chart repository
...Successfully got an update from the "stable" chart repository
Update Complete.  Happy Helming!
```

Let's start with one of the simplest applications available in my Helm repository, kubeslate. This provides some very basic information about your cluster, such as the version of Kubernetes you are running and the number of pods, deployments, and services in your cluster. We are going to start with this application, since it is very simple and doesn't require any special configuration to run on Minikube, or indeed any other cluster.

Installing a chart from a repository on your cluster couldn't be simpler:

```
$ helm install --name=my-slate errm/kubeslate
```

You should see a lot of output from the helm command.

Firstly, you will see some metadata about the release, such as its name, status, and namespace:

```
NAME:   my-slate
LAST DEPLOYED: Mon Mar 26 21:55:39 2018
NAMESPACE: default
STATUS: DEPLOYED
```

Next, you should see some information about the resources that Helm has instructed Kubernetes to create on the cluster. As you can see, a single service and a single deployment have been created:

```
RESOURCES:
==> v1/Service
NAME                   TYPE        CLUSTER-IP      PORT(S)   AGE
my-slate-kubeslate     ClusterIP   10.100.209.48   80/TCP    0s
==> v1/Deployment
NAME                   DESIRED   CURRENT   UP-TO-DATE   AVAILABLE   AGE
my-slate-kubeslate     2         0         0            0           0s
==> v1/Pod(related)
NAME                                        READY   STATUS             AGE
my-slate-kubeslate-77bd7479cf-gckf8   0/1     ContainerCreating   0s
my-slate-kubeslate-77bd7479cf-vvlnz 0/1 ContainerCreating 0s
```

Finally, there is a section with some notes that have been provided by the chart's author to give us some information about how to start using the application:

> **Notes**:
>
> To access `kubeslate`.
>
> 1. First start the kubectl proxy:
>
>   **kubectl proxy**
>
> 2. Now open the following URL in your browser:
>
>   `http://localhost:8001/api/v1/namespaces/default/se`
>   `rvices/my-slate-kubeslate:http/proxy`
>
> Please try reloading the page if you see `ServiceUnavailable / no`
> `endpoints available for service,` as pod creation might take a few
> moments.

Try following these instructions yourself and open Kubeslate in your browser:

Kubeslate deployed with Helm

Configuring a chart

When you use Helm to make a release of a chart, there are certain attributes that you might need to change, or configuration you might need to provide. Luckily, Helm provides a standard way for users of a chart to override some or all of the configuration values.

In this section, we are going to look at how, as the user of a chart, you might go about supplying configuration to Helm. Later in the chapter, we are going to look at how you can create your own charts and use the configuration passed in to allow your chart to be customized.

When we invoke `helm install`, there are two ways we can provide configuration values: passing them as command-line arguments, or by providing a configuration file.

These configuration values are merged with the default values provided by a chart. This allows a chart author to provide a default configuration to allow users to get up and running quickly, but still allow users to tweak important settings, or enable advanced features.

Providing a single value to Helm on the command line is achieved by using the set flag. The `kubeslate` chart allows us to specify additional labels for the pod(s) that it launches using the `podLabels` variable. Let's make a new release of the kubeslate chart, and then use the `podLabels` variable to add an additional `hello` label with the value `world`:

```
$ helm install --name labeled-slate --set podLabels.hello=world
errm/kubeslate
```

Once you have run this command, you should be able to prove that the extra variable you passed to Helm did indeed result in the pods launched by Helm having the correct label. Using the `kubectl get pods` command with a label selector for the label we applied using Helm should return the pods that have just been launched with Helm:

```
$ kubectl get pods -l hello=world
NAME                                     READY     STATUS
labeled-slate-kubeslate-5b75b58cb-7jpfk  1/1       Running
labeled-slate-kubeslate-5b75b58cb-hcpgj  1/1       Running
```

As well as being able to pass a configuration to Helm when we create a new release, it is also possible to update the configuration in a pre-existing release using the upgrade command. When we use Helm to update a configuration, the process is much the same as when we updated deployment resources in the last chapter, and a lot of those considerations still apply if we want to avoid downtime in our services. For example, by launching multiple replicas of a service, we can avoid downtime, as a new version of a deployment configuration is rolled out.

Let's also upgrade our original kubeslate release to include the same `hello: world` pod label that we applied to the second release. As you can see, the structure of the `upgrade` command is quite similar to the `install` command. But rather than specifying the name of the release with the `--name` flag, we pass it as the first argument. This is because when we install a chart to the cluster, the name of the release is optional. If we omit it, Helm will create a random name for the release. However, when performing an upgrade, we need to target a pre-existing release to upgrade, and thus this argument is mandatory:

```
$ helm upgrade my-slate --set podLabels.hello=world errm/kubeslate
```

If you now run `helm ls`, you should see that the release named `my-slate` has been upgraded to Revision 2. You can test that the deployment managed by this release has been upgraded to include this pod label by repeating our `kubectl get` command:

```
$ kubectl get pods -l hello=world
NAME                                       READY      STATUS
labeled-slate-kubeslate-5b75b58cb-7jpfk    1/1        Running
labeled-slate-kubeslate-5b75b58cb-hcpgj    1/1        Running
my-slate-kubeslate-5c8c4bc77-4g4l4         1/1        Running
my-slate-kubeslate-5c8c4bc77-7pdtf         1/1        Running
```

We can now see that four pods, two from each of our releases, now match the label selector we passed to `kubectl get`.

Passing variables on the command line with the `set` flag is convenient when we just want to provide values for a few variables. But when we want to pass more complex configurations, it can be simpler to provide the values as a file. Let's prepare a configuration file to apply several labels to our kubeslate pods:

```
values.yml
podLabels:
  hello: world
  access: internal
  users: admin
```

We can then use the `helm` command to apply this configuration file to our release:

```
$ helm upgrade labeled-slate -f values.yml errm/kubeslate
```

Creating your own charts

Now you have a little experience with Helm and can use the command-line tool to install a chart from a community repository, we are going to take a look at how you can leverage Helm to build charts for your own applications.

We will walk through using Helm to deploy the versions application that we manually deployed in Chapter 4, *Managing Change in Your Applications*. The aim here is for us to replicate the deployments we made in Chapter 4, *Managing Change in Your Applications*, but this time to encapsulate the configuration in a Helm chart so it is simple to make configuration changes, deploy new versions of our code, and even deploy the same configuration multiple times.

Helm makes it very easy to build a chart and deploy it to your cluster. The Helm command-line tool has some commands that will get us started very quickly. The helm create command will create a skeleton for our new chart that we can quickly fill in with the configuration for our application:

```
$ helm create version-app
Creating version-app
$ tree version-app
version-app
├──── Chart.yaml
├──── values.yaml
└──── templates
      ├──── NOTES.txt
      ├──── _helpers.tpl
      ├──── deployment.yaml
      └──── service.yaml
2 directories, 7 files
```

Let's look at each of the files created by Helm, and then look at the configuration we will need to add to deploy our versioned web service from Chapter 4, *Managing Change in Your Applications*.

Chart.yaml

This file contains some basic metadata about this chart, such as its name, a description, and a version number. This file is required.

values.yaml

This file contains the default configuration values for this chart. These are the values that will be used when rendering the templated resources when installing the chart, unless overrides are provided.

templates

This directory contains the templates that will be rendered to produce the definitions of the resources that this chart provides. When we run the `helm new` command, several skeleton template files are created for us.

`NOTES.txt` is a special file that is used to provide a post-install message to users of your chart. You saw an example of this earlier in the chapter when we installed the kube-ops-dashboard.

As with the YAML resources we created by hand in earlier chapters, Helm doesn't attach any significance to the filenames we give to our resources. It is up to you to decide how to organize resources within the templates directory. The skeleton chart we created just now comes with a few files to get us started, but if you need to create more resources, you may just add additional files to the templates directory.

`deployment.yaml` contains a simple manifest for a deployment, `service.yaml` contains a simple service manifest for this deployment, and `_helpers.tpl` contains some predefined helper functions that you can reuse throughout your chart.

When you ran `helm new`, some other files may have been created. These are optional files used for some more advanced functionality, and we can ignore them for now, but if you wish, you can safely remove them altogether from your chart.

There are some standard ways of working with the templates directory that are followed in the community charts repository. You might like to review these, as they do help to keep your work organized. But unless you are planning to try getting your chart published to the community repository, there is no need to stick rigidly to these guidelines: `https://docs.helm.sh/chart_best_practices`.

Making it your own

Let's go through the steps that we will take to edit this chart in order to deploy our own application. Start by taking a look at the generated deployment.yaml file. You will notice that it looks very similar to the manifest that we produced in Chapter 4, *Managing Change in Your Applications*, but with one important difference: all of the specific configuration values have replaced will calls to variables. Look, for example, at the line where the image for the container is specified:

```
image: "{{ .Values.image.repository }}:{{ .Values.image.tag }}"
```

You will notice that when a reference to a variable is inserted into the template, it is surrounded by two curly braces, like this: {{ variable }}. Secondly, you will also notice the dot notation used to access nested attributes on objects. The .Values object refers to all of the values, either supplied (by default) from the values.yaml file within the chart, or overridden from the command line when the chart is deployed.

So, in order to configure the source for the image we want to use in our deployment, let's start by editing the values.yaml file. Find the section where the image is configured and edit to pull the versions application we deployed in Chapter 4, *Managing Change in Your Applications*:

```
image:
  repository: errm/versions
  tag: 0.0.1
  pullPolicy: IfNotPresent
```

While we are editing the values.yaml file, let's also edit the values used to configure the service that Helm created for our deployment. We need to change the port that our container exposes from 80 to 3000, and we should change the name of our service from nginx to something more descriptive:

```
service:
  name: versions
  type: ClusterIp
  externalPort: 80
  internalPort: 3000
```

If we go back and look at `deployment.yaml` and `service.yaml`, we can see one of the advantages of being able to inject variables into our Kubernetes resources with templates.

By changing the value of `service.internalPort` in the `values.yaml` file, we have a single source of truth; in this case, the port that our container exposes. This single source of truth then gets used three times within `deployment.yaml` and then again in `service.yaml`. Of course, with a simple example like this, we could have edited these files manually, but it makes the cost of maintaining the configuration that little bit higher, having to search through several resources, and understanding how different configuration values interact.

 When I am building a Helm chart, I try to imagine my future self using the chart. My aim is to expose enough variables to make the chart flexible enough to reuse and redeploy in several environments without having to change or even look at the templates. To achieve this, it is important to choose descriptive variable names, and provide clear documentation for the use of those variables in the `README.md` file.

It is simple to deploy our chart using the Helm command-line client, rather than referring to the name of a chart within a remote repository (for example, `stable/kube-ops-view`). We can run our Helm commands by pointing to the chart directory on disk:

```
$ helm install --name happy-bear version-app/
NAME:   happy-bear
LAST DEPLOYED: Sun Dec  3 13:22:13 2017
NAMESPACE: default
STATUS: DEPLOYED
RESOURCES:
==> v1/Service
NAME                     TYPE        CLUSTER-IP   EXTERNAL-IP   PORT(S)
happy-bear-version-app   ClusterIP   10.0.0.121   <none>        80/TCP
==> v1/Deployment
NAME                     DESIRED   CURRENT   UP-TO-DATE   AVAILABLE
happy-bear-version-app   1         1         1            0
==> v1/Pod(related)
NAME                                     READY   STATUS
happy-bear-version-app-6597799867-ct51k  0/1     ContainerCreating
```

Now the chart has been installed on to our cluster, let's test that it's working correctly. The simplest way to do this is to run `kubectl proxy` to set up a local proxy to the kubernetes API, and use the service endpoint to view our service. The chart that Helm created for us creates a service with a name formed by combining the name of the release with the name of the chart. So, assuming that the `kubectl proxy` started on port `8001`, we should be able to view our service at the following URL:

`http://localhost:8001/api/v1/namespaces/default/services/happy-bear-version-app:80/.`

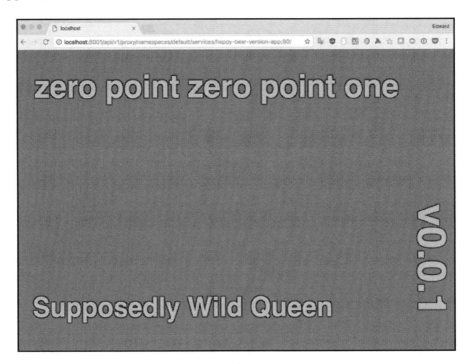

Developing and debugging

As our charts become more complex and we leverage more of the power of the templating language that Helm provides to build our own abstractions on top of the Kubernetes resources, you might notice that it becomes harder to reason about errors returned by Kubernetes. Because we can no longer see the resources directly that we are submitting to Kubernetes, it can become harder to work out the source of a bug or misconfiguration.

Luckily, Helm has some options that will help us debug our charts as we develop them:

- `--dry-run`: This option allows us to submit our chart to the Tiller server, where it will be validated in exactly the same way as when we deploy our chart without actually submitting the resources to Kubernetes. This lets us see and understand any errors with our chart quickly without having to use resources on our cluster.
- `--debug`: This option allows us to see a lot of useful debugging information; in fact, so much that it can be a little overwhelming at first. Firstly, we see some logging information marked `[debug]`. This includes some details about how the Helm client is connecting to Tiller and the chart that is being deployed.

This is followed by the release metadata. This is made up from the chart metadata from `Chart.yaml` and computed information about the release, such as its number and the date and time that it was made.

The next section, `COMPUTED VALUES`, shows the exact values that Helm will be using as it renders the templates to produce the resources for this release. If you are not passing any extra variables when you make your release, this should be identical to the contents of `values.yaml`, but is very useful if you are trying to understand exactly what variables are being used by the templates if you are providing overrides when you invoke Helm. The `HOOKS` section shows the resources that will be created by the Helm hooks mechanism. You will learn a little about hooks later in this chapter.

Finally, the `MANIFEST` section lists out the computed resources, as they will be submitted to Kubernetes. When you are developing chart templates, this is invaluable, for quickly seeing how your chart behaves given different values. You will find that using both these options together with a call to `helm install` or `helm upgrade` is very useful in debugging your charts, as well as for validating your work and building confidence that changes to your chart or values have the desired effect.

Templating language

Helm's templating language is based on the Go templating language. Essentially, Helm provides the standard templating language from the Go programming language, plus some additional functions and the mechanism for making variables available inside of your templates.

You have already seen how to use the templating language to place information into YAML formatted Kubernetes resources. Calls to functions provided by Helm are surrounded by double curly braces, like `{{ this }}`.

If we simply want to include a variable into our template, we can just refer to it by name. Helm namespaces its variables inside of a number of objects that are exposed to the template. You will have already noticed that the values from our `values.yaml` file (as amended by any overwritten variables passed in on the command line) are available in the `.Values` object. In addition to this object, Helm makes further objects available within the template:

- `.Release`: This object describes the release itself, and includes a number of attributes that can be used to customize your resources to their parent release. Commonly, you will use these values to ensure that the resources from this release do not conflict with the resources from another release of the same chart.
- `.Release.Name`: This is the name of the release. It can be passed to `helm install` with the `--name` flag, or it might be automatically generated.
- `.Release.Time.Seconds`: This is the time when the release was created as a UNIX-style timestamp. It can be useful if you need to add a unique value to a resource name.
- `.Release.Namespace`: This indicates the Kubernetes namespace of this release.
- `.Release.Service`: This indicates the service that made the release. Currently, this is always Tiller, but if there was an alternative implementation of Helm, perhaps it would populate this attribute differently.
- `.Release.Revision`: This is a number used to track updates to the release. It begins with 1 and increases each time the release is upgraded via `helm upgrade`.
- `.Release.IsUpgrade` and `.Release.IsInstall`: These are Boolean values that indicate if the operation producing this release is a new install of the chart, or an upgrade of an existing release. These might be utilized to only carry out actions at a particular point in the chart's life cycle.
- `.Chart`: The chart object contains the fields from `Chart.yaml`.
- `.Files`: This object allows you to access the contents of non-template files included in the chart. It exposes two functions, `.Get` and `.GetBytes`, that allow you to read contents of files as text or indeed as bytes. This can be useful for providing static config files or other data that is not included in your container images as part of your chart.

- `.Capabilities`: This object provides information about the cluster that Tiller is running on. It can be useful to query this information if you want to produce a chart that will work with more than one version of Kubernetes. You will see an example of this later in the chapter.
- `.Template`: This object provides a `.Name` and a `.BasePath` attribute that includes the filename and directory of the template currently being rendered by Helm.

Functions

Helm's templating language provides over 60 functions that can manipulate and format the data we pass to our templates.

Some of these functions are part of the Go templating language, but most are part of the Sprig templating language.
When you begin using Helm, it can be useful to have the documentation to hand so you can find the function that you need.

- `https://godoc.org/text/template`
- `https://godoc.org/github.com/Masterminds/sprig`

There are two ways to invoke a template function in the Helm templating language. The first of these involves calling a function, and passing a value as an argument.

For example, `{{ upper "hello" }}` will produce the output `HELLO`.

The second way to invoke a function is as a pipeline. You can think of a pipeline a little like a UNIX pipe; it provides a concise way to pass the result of one function to another. This lets us compose together several functions to get at the result we want.

We could rewrite our first example as `{{ "hello" | upper }}` and the result would be exactly the same. The advantage of this form comes when we want to apply several functions to a value. When we use the pipeline operator, the result of the previous function is passed into the next as the last argument. This allows us to also call functions that take more than one argument, and is the reason that most of the functions in Helm are optimized to take the value to be operated on as the last argument.

We could, for example, form a pipeline with the `trunc` function to truncate our string to a certain number of characters and then use the `upper` function to uppercase the result, like this: `{{ "hello" | trunc 4 | upper }}`. The result, of course, would be `HELL`.

Flow control

We already get a lot of value from Helm by being able to take a single value from a chart and include it in a number of places throughout a chart, like the example earlier in the chapter, where we referred to the same port number in several related places. You might also use this technique, for example, to ensure a system with a number of different components provided by different containers are always deployed to the same version number.

Another important way that we can use variables in our Helm charts is to provide a signal to our template to change our configuration or even turn whole features into optional extras that might not always be enabled.

There are three constructs that allow us to construct really powerful abstractions using Helm templates: `if...else`, `range`, and `with`.

The structure of the `if...else` construct in Helm should be very familiar to anyone who has used a programming language. We use the `if` keyword to test a variable or expression. If the test passes, we do the action in the first branch; if not, we fall back to the action indicated by the `else` branch.

Here is an example you might use to provide a custom message in the `NOTES.txt` template, depending on the value of a variable:

```
{{ if .Values.production }}
WARNING THIS IS A PRODUCTION ENVIRONMENT - do not use for testing.
{{ else }}
THIS IS A TEST ENVIRONMENT; any data will be purged at midnight.
{{ end }}
```

`if` functions can be nested within the `else` branch to provide more complex behavior. In this example, the `Capabilities` object is queried so the templated resource can use a correct API version for a `CronJob` resource. This kind of capability is useful since it lets you make changes to your configuration to support a newer version of Kubernetes, but maintain backwards compatibility. If both of our tests for a supported version fail, then we explicitly throw an error that will halt the installation of the chart:

```
{{- if and ge .Capabilities.KubeVersion.Minor "8" -}}
apiVersion: batch/v1beta1
  {{- else if ge .Capabilities.KubeVersion.Minor "5" -}}
apiVersion: batch/v1alpha1
{{- else -}}
{{required "Kubernetes version 1.5 or higher required" nil }}
{{- end -}}
```

Providing toggles like this around configuration based on feature flags or even version numbers is a very useful tool to manage change in your configuration. It allows you to add an option to your chart, test it out in safety, and then only enable it when you are happy to do so.

The `range` keyword is used to loop over a collection. It can loop over simple lists or collections with a key value structure.

Let's start by adding a list of values to our `values.yaml` file:

```
users:
  - yogi
  - paddington
  - teddy
```

Then we can use the `range` keyword to loop over the data in our list, and use values in our template:

```
apiVersion: v1
kind: ConfigMap
metadata:
  name: {{ .Release.Name }}-configmap
data:
  usernames: |-
    {{- range .Values.users }}
    {{ . }}
    {{- end }}
```

In this example, we are using the `|-` marker, which is part of YAML. It indicates that the usernames string is multi-line. This will result in each username being available in the `ConfigMap` separated by new lines.

As you can see here, when we use the range function on a list, on each iteration, the special `.` variable is replaced by the value from the list.

When rendered, this template produces the following result:

```
apiVersion: v1
kind: ConfigMap
metadata:
  name: ordered-dolphin-configmap
data:
  usernames: |-
    yogi
    paddington
    teddy
```

In this next example, we are going to assign the result of the range function to two variables. When we do this with a list, the first variable includes an index, and you will notice that when we assign a variable, we prefix its name with a $:

```
apiVersion: v1
kind: ConfigMap
metadata:
  name: {{ .Release.Name }}-configmap
data:
  user_id.properties: |-
    {{- range $index, $user := .Values.users }}
    user.{{ $user }}={{ $index }}
    {{- end }}
```

The output of this template when rendered looks like this:

```
apiVersion: v1
kind: ConfigMap
metadata:
  name: interested-ibex-configmap
data:
  user_id.properties: |-
    user.yogi.id=0
    user.paddington.id=1
    user.teddy.id=2
```

When using the range function to loop over a key value structure, we can also use variables to capture the key and the value.

Let's consider the following data in our `values.yaml` file:

```
users:
  yogi:
    food: picnic
    height: 1500
  paddington:
    food: marmalade
    height: 1066
  teddy:
    food: honey
    height: 500
```

Now we have some key value data in the users variable, let's use it to configure some environment variables for a pod:

```
apiVersion: v1
kind: Pod
metadata:
```

```
    name: {{ .Release.Name }}-env-pod
spec:
  containers:
  - image: alpine
    name: bear-env
    env:
    {{- range $name, $user := .Values.users }}
      {{- range $var, $value := $user }}
      - name: {{ $name | upper }}_BEAR_{{ $var | upper }}
        value: {{ $value | quote }}
      {{- end }}
    {{- end }}
    command: ["env"]
```

When we use the range keyword to loop over a key value structure, the key becomes the first variable returned and the value becomes the second. By nesting loops, as in this case, it becomes possible to use quite complex data structures in the values file.

> The type of some variables in Kubernetes resources is important. In the preceding example, the value in an environment variable must always be a string, so we have used the `quote` pipeline function to ensure that values of other types (like numbers) are of the correct string type.

When rendered, this template produces a pod manifest, like this:

```
apiVersion: v1
kind: Pod
metadata:
  name: solemn-whale-env-pod
spec:
  containers:
  - image: alpine
    name: bear-env
    env:
      - name: PADDINGTON_BEAR_FOOD
        value: "marmalade"
      - name: PADDINGTON_BEAR_HEIGHT
        value: "1066"
      - name: TEDDY_BEAR_FOOD
        value: "honey"
      - name: TEDDY_BEAR_HEIGHT
        value: "500"
      - name: YOGI_BEAR_FOOD
        value: "picnic"
      - name: YOGI_BEAR_HEIGHT
        value: "1500"
    command: ["env"]
```

Hooks

So far, we have been using Helm to help us generate the resources our applications need to be submitted to Kubernetes. In the ideal world, this would be all that we would need a tool like Helm to do. Kubernetes aims to be declarative; in other words, we submit resources describing what we want the state of the cluster to look like, and Kubernetes handles the rest.

Unfortunately, in the real world, sometimes we still need to explicitly take some actions to get our applications running correctly. Perhaps when you install your application, you need to run a script to initialize a database schema or set up some default users. Perhaps when you install a new version of an application, you need to run a script to migrate the schema of your database to be compatible with the new version of the application.

Helm provides a hook mechanism that allows us to take actions at eight specific points in the life cycle of a release. In order to define a hook in your Helm chart, you add the `helm.sh/hook` annotation to a resource. You can use the hook annotation on any resource to ensure that it is created at the appropriate time. But typically, it is very useful to create resources of the job type. If your resource is of the job type, Tiller will block until the job has successfully run to completion. This means that if you are using one of the `pre-` hooks then your application can depend on that job having run.

- `pre-install`: This action runs after Tiller has rendered the templates in a chart, but before any resources have been submitted to the Kubernetes API. This action runs when a new release is created by installing a chart. If you also need a hook to run when a release is upgraded, you should combine this hook with the `pre-upgrade` hook. You might make use of this hook to initialize resources that will be used by your application.
- `post-install`: This action runs after all the resources have been submitted to the Kubernetes API. You might, for example, use this to run a script that provides notifications to a chatroom or to register the new instance of the chart with a monitoring tool.
- `pre-delete`: This hook runs before any resources are deleted from Kubernetes when a deletion request is made. This could be useful, for example, if you needed to make a backup of data stored by your application.
- `post-delete`: This hook runs after Helm has deleted the resources created as part of a release. You might utilize this hook to clean up any external resources that your application uses that are not managed by Helm or Kubernetes.

- `pre-upgrade`: This hook provides the same functionality as the `pre-install` hook, but runs each time a release is upgraded. You might use this hook to run a database migration script.
- `post-upgrade`: This hook provides the same functionality as the `post-install` hook, but runs each time a release is upgraded. Again, this might be used for notification purposes.
- `pre-rollback`: This hook runs before changes to rollback an upgrade of a release is submitted to the Kubernetes API.
- `post-rollback`: This hook runs after a request to rollback an upgrade of the release has been submitted to Kubernetes. Depending on the expectations of your application, you might run scripts to roll back database changes here or in the `pre-rollback` hook.
- Let's look at an example, where we will be using a hook to run a setup script:

```
apiVersion: batch/v1
kind: Job
metadata:
  name: "{{.Release.Name}}-setup"
  labels:
    heritage: {{.Release.Service | quote }}
    release: {{.Release.Name | quote }}
    chart: "{{.Chart.Name}}-{{.Chart.Version}}"
  annotations:
    "helm.sh/hook": pre-install
spec:
  template:
    metadata:
      name: "{{.Release.Name}}-setup"
    labels:
      heritage: {{.Release.Service | quote }}
      release: {{.Release.Name | quote }}
      chart: "{{.Chart.Name}}-{{.Chart.Version}}"
    spec:
      restartPolicy: Never
      containers:
      - name: setup
        image: errm/awesome-application
        command: ["bin/setup"]
```

Everything about the definition of this job is the same as the standard Kubernetes resource definition that we looked at in `Chapter 4`, *Managing Change in Your Applications*. It is the annotation added to the job metadata that enables Helm to treat this definition as a hook rather than a managed part of our application.

A single resource can be used to implement multiple hooks. For example, if you wanted the setup script to be run each time the release is updated as well as when it is first installed, we could change the hook annotation to:

```
annotations:
  "helm.sh/hook": pre-install,pre-upgrade
```

Helm allows you to create any Kubernetes resource using the hook mechanism. This might be useful if, for example, a job created using a hook depends on a `ConfigMap` or `Secret`.

If you have multiple hook resources that need to be created in a specific order, you can use the `helm.sh/hook-weight` annotation. This weight can be any positive or negative integer number. When Helm evaluates a particular hook, the resources will be sorted by these weights in ascending order. Since annotations can only hold strings, it is important to quote the number used in a hook weight.

For example, a resource with the annotation `"helm.sh/hook-weight": "-5"` would be run before `"helm.sh/hook-weight": "5"`, but would be run after a resource with the annotation `"helm.sh/hook-weight": "-10"`.

There is one wrinkle in Helm's hook system that can be quite confusing at first, but luckily, once you understand it, there are some simple ways to work around it.

Helm keeps track of nearly all of the resources you create with your templates. This means that when you upgrade a release, Helm can update all of the resources managed by the release, and when a release is deleted, Helm can remove all of the resources that it created. The one exception to this is the resources created by hooks. Once they are created, Helm no longer manages them and Kubernetes takes over.

This can cause two different issues when using them in your charts:

Firstly, when a chart is deleted, the resources created by hooks won't be deleted. This can unexpectedly use up resources in your cluster unless the resources are manually deleted. Secondly, if you are using a hook that can be called more than once in the life of a chart release, the names of your resources can clash.

With our example job, to run a setup script if we had updated the hook annotation to `"helm.sh/hook": pre-install,pre-upgrade`, we would have found that the job would run correctly when the chart was installed, but when we come to upgrade the release, Helm would try to create a new job with the same name as the job already created in the `pre-install` hook. This would cause an error, which would prevent the upgrade from proceeding.

One way to work around this issue would be to include the release revision number in the name of job, as in the following:

```
metadata:
  name: "{{.Release.Name}}-setup-{{ Release.Revision }}"
```

While this does prevent job names from colliding, it does mean that each upgrade of a release will create a new resource, all of which may need to be cleaned up manually when they are no longer required.

Helm provides one more annotation to assist us with this issue. The `helm.sh/hook-delete-policy` allows us to instruct Helm to delete a resource after it has been successfully executed, or after it fails, or both.

The annotation `"helm.sh/hook-delete-policy": hook-succeeded` is useful for the majority of use cases, such as the setup script job example. If the job runs successfully, it is deleted, cleaning up the resource ready for a new instance to be created with the same name the next time the chart is upgraded. If the job fails, it is left as is on the Kubernetes server so it could be inspected for debugging purposes.

If you are using Helm as part of an automated workflow, where it is important to ensure all of the resources created by installing a chart are deleted, whatever the outcome, you might want to use the following annotation:

```
"helm.sh/hook-delete-policy": hook-succeeded,hook-failed
```

Packaging Helm charts

While we are developing our chart, it is simple to use the Helm CLI to deploy our chart straight from the local filesystem. However, Helm also allows you to create your own repository in order to share your charts.

A Helm repository is a collection of packaged Helm charts, plus an index stored in a particular directory structure on a standard HTTP web server.

Once you are happy with your chart, you will want to package it so it is ready to distribute in a Helm repository. This is simple to do with the `helm package` command. When you start to distribute your charts with a repository, versioning becomes important. The version number of a chart in a Helm repository needs to follow the SemVer 2 guidelines.

In order to build a packaged chart, start by checking that you have set an appropriate version number in `Chart.yaml`. If this is the first time you have packaged your chart, the default will be OK:

```
$ helm package version-app
Successfully packaged chart and saved it to: ~/helm-charts/version-
app-0.1.0.tgz
```

You can test a packaged chart without uploading it to a repository by using the `helm serve` command. This command will serve all of the packaged charts found in the current directory and generate an index on the fly:

```
$ helm serve
Regenerating index. This may take a moment.
Now serving you on 127.0.0.1:8879
```

You can now try installing your chart by using the local repository:

```
$ helm install local/version-app
```

You can test building an index

An Helm repository is just a collection of packaged charts stored in a directory. In order to discover and search the charts and versions available in a particular repository, the Helm client downloads a special `index.yaml` that includes metadata about each packaged chart and the location it can be downloaded from.

In order to generate this index file, we need to copy all the packaged charts that we want in our index to the same directory:

```
cp ~/helm-charts/version-app-0.1.0.tgz ~/helm-repo/
```

Then, in order to generate the `index.yaml` file, we use the `helm repo index` command. You will need to pass the root URL where the packaged charts will be served from. This could be the address of a web server, or on AWS, you might use a S3 bucket:

```
helm repo index ~/helm-repo --url https://helm-repo.example.org
```

The chart index is quite a simple format, listing the name of each chart available, and then providing a list of each version available for each named chart. The index also includes a checksum in order to validate the download of charts from the repository:

```
apiVersion: v1
entries:
  version-app:
```

```
  - apiVersion: v1
    created: 2018-01-10T19:28:27.802896842Z
    description: A Helm chart for Kubernetes
    digest:
79aee8b48cab65f0d3693b98ae8234fe889b22815db87861e590276a657912c1
    name: version-app
    urls:
    - https://helm-repo.example.org/version-app-0.1.0.tgz
    version: 0.1.0
generated: 2018-01-10T19:28:27.802428278Z
```

The generated `index.yaml` file for our new chart repository.

Once we have created the `index.yaml` file, it is simply a question of copying your packaged charts and the index file to the host you have chosen to use. If you are using S3, this might look like this:

```
aws s3 sync ~/helm-repo s3://my-helm-repo-bucket
```

In order for Helm to be able to use your repository, your web server (or S3) needs to be correctly configured.
The web server needs to serve the `index.yaml` file with the correct content type header (`text/yaml` or `text/x-yaml`).
The charts need to be available at the URLs listed in the index.

Using your repository

Once you have set up the repository, you can configure Helm to use it:

```
helm repo add my-repo https://helm-repo.example.org
my-repo has been added to your repositories
```

When you add a repository, Helm validates that it can indeed connect to the URL given and download the index file.

You can check this by searching for your chart by using `helm search`:

```
$ helm search version-app
NAME                    VERSION         DESCRIPTION
my-repo/version-app     0.1.1           A Helm chart for Kubernetes
```

Organizational patterns for Helm

Within an organization using Kubernetes to deploy its own applications, there are a few strategies that you might want to consider in order to produce and maintain charts to manage deploying the applications that you use.

Chart per application

The simplest way to use Helm within your organization is to create a new chart for each application that you want to deploy to Kubernetes.

When you have an application that might be deployed to a number of different contexts, such as testing, staging, and production environments, this can make sure that you have parity between each environment while making it simple to provide overrides for the configuration that might be environment-specific.

Creating Helm charts for your applications can help in larger organizations where applications might need to be deployed to a number of different environments without the help of the team that builds and manages the application.

For example, mobile app or frontend web developers might deploy a backend API application developed by another team to a testing or development environment using Helm. If the team that develops the backend provides a Helm chart, they make it simple for other teams to deploy without needing in-depth knowledge of how to install and configure the app.

If the same Helm chart is used to deploy to production as well as the testing and development environments, it is simpler to reduce the otherwise inevitable drift between production and development environments.

It is simple to use the control flow features of the Helm templating language to provide different configurations where appropriate. For example, in staging or production environments, your application might rely on saving data to an EBS volume, whereas on development machines, the application might simply save to a local volume.

You might need to override some values when your chart is deployed. For example, you might want to run many more replicas of a pod in a production environment, whereas on a development machine, a single replica might be sufficient.

If your application can be scaled horizontally by adding more replicas of a pod, it makes sense to provide the same memory and CPU limits in all environments and then scale up for production traffic by adding additional pods, rather than giving each pod greater resource limits. This makes it much simpler to debug issues with applications being killed due to out-of-memory errors or being starved of CPU resources, since a single pod will have the same resources on your development and production clusters.

Shared charts

If your organization maintains a service or micro-service based system, it is common to maintain some level of standardization between the different services that you deploy.

One way of maintaining a consistent pattern of deployment between each of your applications is to provide a Helm chart that can be used to deploy all of your services.

If you do this, you will find that the configuration you need to provide to the chart and the templates themselves becomes more complex. But the advantage of working this way is it lets you quickly apply new configuration best practices to all of your applications.

In the simpler Helm chart, we provided a new template for each pod that would form part of our application. When a chart is to be reused by a number of applications, there might be different pods required by each one.

For example, one application might require a web server and a batch job to run every hour, while another service provides an admin interface and a worker for processing background jobs from a message queue.

To be able to deploy two different applications with these different sorts of pods using one chart, you need to produce a template—not for each pod in your application, but for each type of pod that your service contract supports.

For example, you might have one template for long-running pods that are managed with Kubernetes Deployment Resources, and another template for managing batch jobs with the `CronJob` resource. To then enable and configure each of these templates, you can provide a list of each of the pods that your application requires in the values passed when you deploy your application.

I have made an example chart that takes this approach. It is available at `https://github.com/errm/charts/tree/master/app`.

Library charts

If your organization has configuration and deployment patterns that you want to share between different applications, but the shared chart approach doesn't provide enough flexibility or results in overly complex logic in your templates, one alternative is to provide library charts that include templates or functions that can be used as dependencies of your application to provide common components or configuration to each chart that needs them.

This can provide you with some of the benefits of both approaches through being able to tailor your chart to a specific application, whilst still being able to use shared functionality, to reduce duplication of configuration or to enforce best practices or other organization-wide deployment patterns.

Next steps

Helm is so powerful because it lets you build your own abstractions over a group of Kubernetes resources with very little extra effort. You might need to spend a little time learning how to use the templating language and how to integrate building and updating charts and making and updating releases with your development and release procedures.

Helm can be used for a wide range of scenarios where you want to deploy resources to a Kubernetes cluster, from providing a simple way for others to install an application you have written on their own clusters, to forming the cornerstone of an internal Platform as a Service within a larger organization. Beyond what is included in this chapter, there is a lot more for you to learn.

Helm has excellent documentation that can be accessed at `https://docs.helm.sh/`.

Another great source for learning how to use Helm effectively is the community-maintained charts repository at `https://github.com/helm/charts`. You will find that there a lot of techniques and best practices you can learn by looking at the charts available there.

6
Planning for Production

Kubernetes provides an excellent platform for developers to rapidly build highly flexible distributed applications. By running our applications on Kubernetes, we have a number of tools at our disposal to simplify their operation, and for making them more reliable, resilient to errors, and, ultimately, highly available.

In order for us to depend on some of the guarantees and behaviors that our applications can inherit from Kubernetes, it is important that we understand how Kubernetes behaves, and some of the factors that have an impact on a production system.

It is important as a cluster administrator that you have an understanding of the requirements of the applications you are running, and of the users of those applications.

Having an awareness of the way that Kubernetes behaves in production is key, so it is invaluable to gain some practical experience of running your applications on Kubernetes before you start to serve mission-critical traffic. For example, when GitHub migrated their main application to Kubernetes, they started by moving traffic for internal users to their new Kubernetes-based infrastructure, before switching their main production traffic.

> *"The load from internal users helped us find problems, fix bugs, and start getting comfortable with Kubernetes in production. During this period, we worked to increase our confidence by simulating procedures we anticipated performing in the future, writing runbooks, and performing failure tests."*

> —*Jesse Newland* (https://githubengineering.com/kubernetes-at-github/)

While I can cover some of the things that you are likely to encounter when using Kubernetes on AWS in production, it is important to understand that every application and organization is unique in surprising ways. You should think of Kubernetes as a toolkit that will enable you to build a powerful and flexible environment for your organization. Kubernetes isn't a magic bullet that removes the need for operational expertise; it's a tool that assists you in managing your applications.

The design process

The design process is shown as follows:

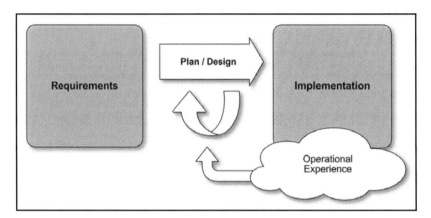

When you think about preparing to use Kubernetes to manage your production infrastructure, you shouldn't think about Kubernetes as your end goal. It is a foundation for building a platform on which to run systems.

When you think about building a platform to meet the needs of the different people in your organization, it becomes much simpler to define the requirements you will place on Kubernetes. When trying to plan for a production environment, you need to understand the requirements that your organization has. Clearly, the technical requirements of the software you want to manage is important. But it is also key to understanding the operational process that your organization needs to support.

Adopting Kubernetes offers a lot of benefits to organizations that have complex requirements for the software that they run. Unfortunately, this complexity can also lead to challenges in safely adopting Kubernetes in a successful way.

Initial planning

You should consider where you will focus your efforts for your initial roll out. You should look for an application that will both deliver valuable results quickly, as well as having a lower risk profile. If we think about the example at GitHub, they initially focused their efforts on building an infrastructure for internal users to quickly test changes to their software. By focusing on a review or staging infrastructure, they found an application for Kubernetes that would both provide value quickly to developers in their organization, as well as an area that had low risks to their business as it was only accessed by internal users.

Applications like these that have a combination of immediate usefulness and a lower impact of downtime are very useful. They allow your organization to gain valuable operational experience using Kubernetes, as well as to drive out bugs and other issues well before you attempt to handle production workloads.

When getting started with Kubernetes, it can be tempting to choose the simplest application that your organization operates and start building processes and tooling around this. However, this can be a mistake because it might lead to you making assumptions about how your applications should be operated, that might make it much harder to later apply the same processes and configuration to more complex applications.

If you choose to start building your platform to support a simple application that doesn't require any backend services, such as a database, you might miss a number of things you need to consider as part of your deployment process. For example, applications that are backed by a database often need to run migration scripts to update the schema when a new version of an application is deployed. If you start by designing a deployment process to meet the needs of a very simple application, you might not surface these requirements until later. Remember, it will always be much simpler to deploy a simple application that only needs a subset of the features that your platform provides, than a more complex application that needs facilities you didn't consider when designing it.

If you choose to focus your efforts on a single application for your initial adoption of Kubernetes, make sure that you choose an application that is representative of your organization's needs. It can be tempting to start using Kubernetes for a greenfield project, as you can take application development decisions with the platform in mind. But remember that a new application may well be significantly simpler than an application that has been in use for a longer time. In the example from GitHub, the application they chose to deploy first was their largest application operated by their organization providing many core services.

If your organization has an application that requires a lot of operational time and effort every time it is deployed, it could be that this would be a good choice for an initial adoption of Kubernetes. Applications like these will be well known for their needs by your development and operational teams, and they will immediately be able to start to utilize Kubernetes to address the issues that previously cost time and effort.

Planning for success

There are a few things that you should try to avoid in order to deliver successfully on a project to adopt Kubernetes.

One trap that can be all too easy to fall into is to change too much too quickly. If you are taking the decision to adopt containerization and Kubernetes, it can be very tempting to adopt a lot of new processes and tools alongside this. This can slow down your progress quite significantly, because what started as a project to run your applications in containers can quickly grow to encompass many other tools and processes that your organization would like to adopt.

You should aim to avoid scope creep and try to change as little as possible in order to deliver your initial adoption of Kubernetes as quickly as possible. It is important to not try to deliver too many of the promises of containerization in one go, as they will hold your adoption back, and may indeed lead to failure of your whole project.

Try to consider the environment you are currently deploying your applications to and aim to replicate its facilities at first, later adding additional functionality. Many of the tools and procedures that we discuss in the rest of this book might indeed be optional for your Kubernetes cluster, items that you can add at a later date to provide additional valuable services, but not to be viewed as blockers to adoption.

If you have the opportunity to reduce the scope of the infrastructure your Kubernetes deployment provides at the time of your additional roll out, you should consider doing so. It reduces the scope of new tools and processes that your organization needs to understand. And it will give you the opportunity to focus on that topic in greater detail at a later time, with reference to the operational experience you will have gained running your applications on Kubernetes.

Consider log management as an example of this—if your current procedure is to log into servers with SSH and tail log files, you can provide the same functionality to operators of your Kubernetes cluster with the `kubectl logs` command. Implementing a solution to aggregate and search logs generated by your cluster might be desirable, but shouldn't necessarily be a blocker to using Kubernetes.

If you currently deploy your applications onto servers running a Linux distribution that is readily available as a container image, you should stick with that distribution, rather than looking for alternatives at this stage, as your developers and operational staff will already be knowledgeable about how it works, and you won't have to invest time fixing incompatibilities. Learning to operate your applications on Kubernetes should be your focus, rather than learning how to configure a new operating system distribution.

Planning for a successful roll out

It can be tempting to shake up the processes and responsibilities in your organization. But trying to do this as part of adopting a new tool like Kubernetes can be risky. For example, if in your organization you have an operations team responsible for deploying and monitoring your applications, the point at which you adopt Kubernetes is not the correct time to hand this responsibility to someone else, such as your development team, or to attempt to automate a manual process.

This can be frustrating because, often, adoption of Kubernetes comes as part of wider plans to improve the processes and tooling that your organization uses. You should wait to successfully establish the use and operation of Kubernetes first. This will put you in a much better position to introduce new tools and processes once you have a stable foundation to build upon. You should view the adoption of Kubernetes as building a foundation that will be flexible enough to implement whatever changes to tools and processes you want to make in the future.

You will discover that implementing new tools, services, and processes becomes much simpler once your application infrastructure is running on Kubernetes. Once you have a Kubernetes cluster at your disposal, you will discover that the barriers to trying out a new tool are significantly reduced. Instead of spending lots of time planning and provisioning, you can quickly evaluate and try out a new tool just by submitting a new configuration to your cluster.

Discovering requirements

The designing requirements are shown in the following diagram:

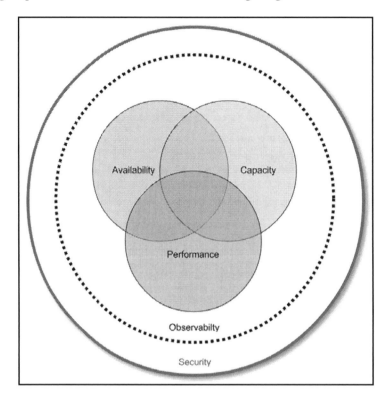

Availability, **capacity**, and **performance** are key properties that we should consider when preparing for production. When gathering the functional requirements for your cluster, it can help to categorize which requirements imply some consideration of these properties.

It is important to understand that it might not be possible to optimize for all three properties without making some trade-offs. For example, for applications that depend on very high network performance, AWS provides a tool called a cluster placement group. This ensures that the best network performance is available by provisioning the EC2 VMs in such a way that fast network interconnections are available between them (presumably by locating them in close proximity within an AWS data center). By provisioning instances this way, the highest network throughputs (above 5 GB) and lowest latencies can be achieved between machines within the cluster placement group. For some applications that require these levels of performance, this might be a worthwhile optimization.

However, since EC2 instances within a cluster placement group cannot span multiple availability zones, reliability of such a setup might be lower, since underlying power or connectivity issues could conceivably affect all the instances in a particular zone, especially if they are deployed in order to maximize interconnect speed. If your application doesn't have a requirement on such high-performance networking, it would indeed be unwise to trade reliability for greater performance.

Overarching these properties is a very important property for a production system—**observability**. Observability really describes the ability for cluster operators to understand what is happening to your applications. Without being able to understand if your applications are performing and behaving as they should, you cannot evaluate, improve, and evolve the design of the system. When designing your cluster, this is the important feedback loop that allows you to maintain and improve your cluster based on operational experience. If you don't consider observability when planning your cluster, it can be much harder to debug issues with the cluster itself and with your applications.

When we are discussing application requirements at a planning stage, it can be hard to understand what the requirements of your applications will be. Having good observability into the performance of your cluster, the underlying hardware, and the applications running on top of it, lets you make pragmatic decisions and be flexible enough to make changes to support your applications as you discover more about how they behave under production workloads and as their functionality is developed over time.

Finally, perhaps the most important property to consider is security. Leaving the security of your cluster to the end of the planning process is a mistake. Remember that although security alone won't lead to the success of your project, failure to secure your cluster could lead to catastrophic consequences.

Recent studies and disclosures have shown that unsecured Kubernetes clusters have already become an attractive target to those who would exploit your computing power for the likes of cryptocurrency mining and other nefarious purposes, not to mention the potential of access to your cluster being used to access sensitive data held within your organization.

Security should be considered and monitored throughout the life cycle of your cluster; indeed, you should try and understand the security implications of each and every other requirement. You will need to consider how members of your organization need to interact with Kubernetes, as well as having a plan to ensure that you secure the configuration and software of your cluster and the applications that you run on it.

In the following sections of this chapter, we will introduce some ideas to help you understand the considerations that you might need to take with regard to these properties. Hopefully, this chapter should give you enough understanding to discover what your requirements are, and to begin planning your cluster for production. For the specific knowledge you will need to implement your plan, keep reading; the second half of this book is almost entirely focused on the practical knowledge you will need to implement your plans.

Availability

The availability is shown in the following diagram:

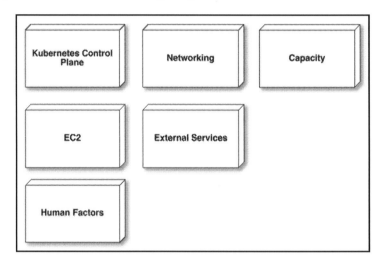

One of the most important things to think about when planning a production system is availability. It is almost always the case that we run software in order to provide our users with a service. If, for whatever reason, our software is not available to meet the requests our users put on it, then, often, we fail to meet their expectations. Depending on the service that your organization provides, unavailability could cause your users to be unhappy, inconvenienced, or even suffer losses or harm. Part of making an adequate plan for any production system is understanding how downtime or errors might affect your users.

Your definition of availability can depend on the sorts of workload that your cluster is running and your business requirements. A key part in planning a Kubernetes cluster is to understand the requirements that the users have for the services you are running.

Consider, for example, a batch job that emails a business report to your users once a day. So long as you can ensure that it runs at least once a day, at roughly the correct time, you can consider it 100% available, whereas a web server that can be accessed by your users at any time of the day or night needs to be available and error-free whenever your users need to access it.

The CEO of your organization will be happy when they arrive at work at 9 a.m. with a report in their inbox ready to read. They won't care that the task failed to run at midnight and was retried a few minutes later successfully. However, if the application server hosting the web mail application that they use to read email is unavailable even for a moment during the day, they may be interrupted and inconvenienced:

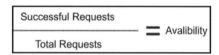

A simple formula to calculate the availability of a service

Generally, systems engineers consider availability of a given service to be the percentage of requests that were successful out of the total requests made to/of the service.

We can consider a batch job that fails even several times to be available. The request we are making of the system (that the report is emailed to the correct person once a day) only requires the job to be completed successfully at least once. If we handle failures gracefully by retrying, there is no impact on our users.

The exact number that you should plan for your systems to meet is, of course, largely a question of the needs of your users, and the priorities of your organization. It is worth bearing in mind, however, that systems designed for higher availability are almost invariably more complex and require more resources than a similar system where periods of downtime are acceptable. As a service approaches 100% availability, the cost and complexity of achieving the additional reliability increases exponentially.

If you don't already know them, it is reasonable to initiate a discussion about availability requirements within your organization. You should do this in order to set targets and understand the best ways to run your software with Kubernetes. Here are some questions that you should try to answer:

- *Do you know how your users are accessing your service?* For example, if your users are using mobile devices then connection to the internet is likely to be more unreliable anyway, masking the uptime (or otherwise) of your service.
- If you are migrating your service to Kubernetes, *do you know how reliable it currently is?*
- *Are you able to put a monetary value on unavailability?* For example, e-commerce or ad-tech organizations will know the exact amount that will be lost for a period of downtime.
- *What levels of unavailability are your users prepared to accept? Do you have competitors?*

You might have noticed that all of these questions are about your users and your organization; there is no solid technical answer to any of them, but you need to be able to answer them to understand the requirements on the system you are building.

In order to provide a highly available service accessed on a network, such as a web server, we need to ensure that the service is available to respond to requests whenever required. Since we cannot ensure that the underlying machines our service is running upon are 100% reliable, we need to run multiple instances of our software and route traffic only to those instances that are able to respond to requests.

The semantics of this batch job imply that (within reason) we are not too concerned about the amount of time the job takes to execute, whereas the time a web server takes to respond is quite significant. There have been many studies that show even sub-second delays added to the length of time a web page takes to load have a significant and measurable impact on users. So, even if we are able to hide failures (for example, by retrying failed requests), we have much lower leeway, and indeed we might even consider high priority requests to have failed if they take longer than a particular threshold.

One reason you might choose to run your applications on Kubernetes is because you have heard about its self-healing properties. Kubernetes will manage our applications and will take action when required to ensure that our applications continue to run in the way that we have requested of Kubernetes. This is a helpful effect of Kubernetes declarative approach to configuration.

With Kubernetes, we would ask for a certain number of replicas of a service to be running on the cluster. The control plane is able to take action to ensure that this condition continues to be true even if something occurs to affect the running application, whether it is due a node failing or instances of an application being killed periodically due to a memory leak.

Contrast this to an imperative deployment procedure that relies on the operator to choose a particular underlying machine (or set of machines) to run an application on. If a machine fails, or even if an instance of the application misbehaves, then manual intervention is required. We want to provide our users with the services that they need without interruption.

For always on or latency sensitive applications such as webservers, Kubernetes provides mechanisms for us to run multiple replicas of our applications and to test the health of our services so that failing instances can be removed from the services or even restarted.

For batch jobs, Kubernetes will retry failed jobs, and will reschedule them to other nodes if the underlying node fails. These semantics of restarting and rescheduling failed applications rely on the Kubernetes control plane to function. Once a pod is running on a particular node, it will continue to run until the following happens:

- It exits
- It is killed by the kubelet for using too much memory
- The API server requests for it to be killed (perhaps to rebalance the cluster or to make way for a pod with a higher priority)

This means that the control plane itself can become temporarily unavailable without affecting the applications running on the cluster. But no pods that have failed, or that were running on a node that has failed, will be rescheduled until the control plane is available again. Clearly, you also need the API server to be available in order to interact with it, so the needs of your organization to push a new configuration to the cluster (for example, to deploy a new version of an application) should also be considered.

We will discuss some strategies and tools that you might use to provide a highly available control plane in `Chapter 7`, *A Production-Ready Cluster*.

Capacity

The capacity is shown in the following diagram:

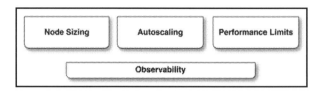

Running a system such as Kubernetes means that you can respond to additional demand for your services literally within the time it takes for your applications to start up. This process can even become automated with tools such as the **Horizontal Pod Autoscaler** (which we we will discuss in Chapter 8, *Sorry My App Ate the Cluster*).

When we couple this flexibility with the ability for us to launch new EC2 instances at will, capacity planning is much less involved than it might have been in the past. Kubernetes and AWS allow us to build applications that only consume the amount of resources that they need to be using at any given time. Rather than anticipating demand for our application and pre-committing to use resources, we can react to the usage requirements of our applications. Kubernetes finally allows us to deliver one of the promises of cloud computing: the promise that we will only pay for the resources that we use.

There are a few considerations that you should take into account in order to make the most efficient use of the resources that you pay to use on AWS.

EC2 instance types

When preparing to launch a Kubernetes cluster, you will probably be drawn into thinking about the type and size of the instances that will make up your cluster. The instances that you choose can have a big impact on the utilization, performance, and cost of operating a Kubernetes cluster.

When Kubernetes schedules your pods to the worker nodes in a cluster, it considers the resource requests and limits that are part of a pod definition.

Typically, your pod specification will request a number of CPUs (or fractions thereof) and a quantity of memory. On AWS, Kubernetes uses AWS's vCPU as its unit of measure. A vCPU (on most instance types) is a single CPU (hyper) thread rather than a CPU core. If you request a fractional number of CPUs then Kubernetes allocates your pod a share of a vCPU. Memory is requested in bytes.

EC2 instances come in several different types that offer different ratios of CPU to memory.

EC2 instance types

The EC2 instance types is shown in the following table:

Category	Type	CPU to memory ratio: vCPU:GiB	Notes
Burstable	T3	1 CPU : 2 GiB	Provides 5-40% CPU baseline + burstable extra use.
CPU optimized	C5	1 CPU : 2 GiB	
General purpose	M5	1 CPU : 4 GiB	
Memory optimized	R5	1 CPU : 8 GiB	
	X1	1 CPU : 15GiB	
	X1e	1 CPU : 30GiB	
You should only consider the following instance types if you need the additional extra resources they provide (GPUs and/or local storage):			
GPU	P3	1 CPU : 7.6GiB	1 GPU : 8 CPU (NVIDIA Tesla V100)
	P2	1 CPU : 4GiB	i. 1 GPU : 4 CPU (NVIDIA K80)
Storage	H1	1 CPU : 4GiB	2TB HDD : 8 CPU
	D2	1 CPU : 7.6GiB	3TB HDD : 2 CPU
	I3	1 CPU : 7.6GiB	475GiB SSD : 2 CPU

When preparing a cluster, we should think about the instance types and size of instances that make up our cluster.

When Kubernetes schedules our pods to the nodes in our cluster, it is of course aiming to pack as many containers as it can onto the cluster. This can be thwarted, however, if the ratio of CPU to memory requests in the majority of our pods is significantly different from the underlying nodes.

For example, consider a scenario where we deploy pods that request 1 CPU and 2 GiB of memory to our cluster. If our cluster were made up of m5.xlarge instances (4 vCPU and 16 GiB memory), each of our nodes would be able to run four pods. Once these four pods are running on this node, no more pods would be able to be scheduled to the node, but half the memory would be unused, effectively stranded.

If your workloads are quite homogeneous, of course it is quite simple to work out what instance type will offer the best ratio of CPU to memory to your applications. However, most clusters run a whole number of applications, each requiring different amounts of memory and CPU (and perhaps even other resources too).

In Chapter 8, *Sorry My App Ate the Cluster*, we discuss using the cluster autoscaler to automatically add and remove instances from AWS autoscaling groups in order to size your cluster to match the requirements of your cluster at any given time. We also discuss how you can use the cluster autoscaler to scale clusters with multiple different instance types, in order to combat the problem of matching the ratio of CPU to memory in clusters where the size and shape of the workloads that are run is quite dynamic and can change from time to time.

Breadth versus depth

Amazon offers many instance sizes for each family; for example, the m5 and c5 families have six different instance sizes available, and each step up offers twice the resources. So, the largest instances have 48 times more resources than the smallest. *How should we choose what size instances to build our cluster with?*

- The size of your instances limits the largest pod you can run on your cluster. The instance needs 10-20% larger than your largest pod to account for the overhead of system services, such as logging or monitoring tools, Docker, and Kubernetes itself.
- Smaller instances will allow you to scale your cluster in smaller increments, increasing utilization.
- Fewer (larger) instances may be simpler to manage.
- Larger instances may use a lower proportion of resources for cluster-level tasks, such as log shipping, and metrics.
- If you want to use monitoring or logging tools, such as Datadog, Sysdig, NewRelic, and so on, where pricing is based on a per instance model, fewer larger instances may be more cost effective.
- Larger instances can provide more disk and networking bandwidth, but if you are running more processes per instance this may not offer any advantage.
- Larger instance sizes are less likely to suffer from noisy neighbor issues at the hypervisor level.
- Larger instances often imply more colocation of your pods. This is usually advantageous when the aim is to increase utilization, but can sometimes cause unexpected patterns of resource limitations.

Performance

The key components of your cluster that impact performance are shown in the following diagram:

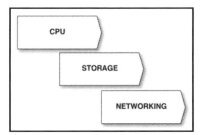

Disk performance

If some of your applications depend on disk performance, understanding the performance characteristics of EBS volumes attached to your instances can become very useful.

All of the current generation of EC2 instances relies on EBS storage. EBS storage is effectively a shared network attached storage, so performance can be affected by a number of factors.

If your cluster is running on the most recent generation of EC2 instances, you will be using EBS optimization. This means that dedicated bandwidth is available for I/O operations on your EBS volumes, effectively eliminating contention between EBS and other network activity.

The total maximum bandwidth available to EBS volumes is determined by the size of the EC2 instance. In a system where you are running multiple containers, potentially with one or more EBS volumes attached to each, you should have an awareness of this upper limit that applies to the aggregate of all volumes in use on an instance.

 If you are planning to run workloads that expect to do large amounts of disk I/O, you may need to consider the total I/O available to the instance.

EBS provides four volume types based on two basic technologies. `gp2` and `io2` volumes are based on SSD, or solid-state drive, technology, while st1 and sc1 volumes are based upon HDD, or hard disk drive technology.

This variety of disks is useful to us because, broadly, we can divide the workloads that your applications might deliver into two groups. Firstly, those that will need to make rapid random reads and/or writes to the filesystem. Workloads that fall into this category include databases, web servers, and boot volumes. With these workloads, the limiting factor for performance is usually **I/O operations per second (IOPS)**. Secondly, there are workloads that need to make sequential reads from the disk as fast as possible. This includes applications such as Map Reduce, Log Management, and datastores, such as Kafka or Casandra, that have been specifically optimized to make sequential reads and writes as much as possible.

There are hard upper limits at the instance level to the maximum performance you can achieve with EBS volumes. The maximum IOPS available to all EBS volumes attached to a single instance is 64,000 on the largest instance size available on c5 and m5 instances. The smallest c5 and m5 instances only provide 1,600 IOPS. It is worth bearing these limits in mind, either if you want to run workloads requiring the higher levels of disk performance on smaller EC2 instance types or are using multiple EBS volumes on the larger instance types.

gp2

gp2 EBS volumes should be your first port of call for most general-purpose applications. They provide **solid-state drive (SSD)** performance at a modest price point. Performance on gp2 volumes is based on a credit system. The volumes provide a baseline performance, and also accrue credits over time that allow performance bust up to 3,000 IOPS when required until the accrued credits are exhausted.

When a gp2 volume is created, it automatically receives a credit balance that allows it to burst up to 3,000 IOPS for 30 minutes. This is very useful when a volume is used as a boot volume or can provide better performance where data needs to be copied rapidly to the volume as part of a bootstrapping procedure.

The rate at which burst credits accrue and the baseline performance of a gp2 volume is proportional to the volume size. Volumes smaller than 33 GiB will always have a minimum baseline performance of 100 IOPS. Volumes larger than 1 TB have a baseline performance greater than 3,000 IOPS, so you won't need to consider burst credits. The maximum performance available to a single gp2 volume is 10,000 IOPS for volumes of 3.3 TB (and larger).

If you have a workload that requires more performance from a gp2 volume, a quick fix can be to use a larger volume (even if your application does not require the storage it provides).

You can calculate what the maximum throughput volume will support by multiplying the IOPS by the block size (256 KiB). However, gp2 volumes limit the total throughput to 160 MiB/s so volumes larger than 214 GiB will only provide 160 MiB/s.

Having the facility to monitor metrics as they relate to disk usage can be invaluable for understanding how disk performance is affecting your applications, and to identify if and where you are hitting performance limits.

io2

For applications where reliable performance is mission critical and gp2 volumes simply cannot provide enough IOPS, io2 volumes (otherwise known as provisioned IOPS volumes) are available. Where the instance they are attached to can support them, io2 volumes can be provisioned to provide a maximum of 32,000 IOPS. When an io2 instance is created, the IOPS required are specified upfront (we will discuss how to do this with Kubernetes in Chapter 9, *Storing State*). The maximum IOPS that can be provisioned for a single volume are dependent on the size of the volume, with the ratio between IOPS and GiB of storage being 50:1. Thus, in order to provision the maximum IOPS, you need to request a volume of at least 640 GiB.

For situations where the required number of IOPS is less than gp2 volumes will support (10,000) and where the required throughput is less that 160 MiB/s, gp2 volumes supporting similar performance characteristics will typically be less than half the price of an io2 volume. Unless you know you have a need for the enhanced performance characteristics of io2 volumes, it makes sense to stick to gp2 volumes for most general-purpose use.

st1

For applications that have be optimized for sequential reads, where the primary performance metric to be concerned about is throughput, it might be surprising given the current dominance of SSDs to note that the best performance is still provided by spinning magnetic disks.

st1 (and **sc1**) volumes are the newest types of EBS volumes available on AWS. They have been designed to offer high throughput for workloads, such as Map Reduce, log processing, data warehousing, and streaming workloads, such as Kafka. st1 volumes offer throughputs of up to 500 MiB/s at less than half the cost of gp2 instances. The downside is that they support much lower IOPS and so offer much worse performance for random or small writes. The IOPS calculations that you might make for SSD are slightly different because the block size is much larger (1 MB versus 256 KB). So, making a small write will take just as long as writing a full 1 MB block (if written sequentially).

Where your workload is correctly optimized to take advantage of the performance characteristics of st1 volumes, it is well worth considering their use because the cost is roughly half that of gp2 volumes.

Just like gp2 volumes, st1 uses a bust bucket model for performance. However, the accumulated credits allow the throughput to burst above the baseline performance. The baseline performance and rate at which credits accumulate are proportional to volume size. With the maximum burst performance being 500 MiB/s for volumes larger than 2 TiB and the maximum baseline performance being 500 MiB/s for volumes larger than 12.5 TiB, for volumes this size (or larger) there is no need to consider burst characteristics since performance is constant.

sc1

`sc1` volumes offer the lowest cost block storage available on AWS. They provide a similar performance profile to `st1` volumes, but roughly half as fast, and for half the cost. You might consider them for applications where you need to store and retrieve data from the filesystem, but access is more infrequent, or performance is not so important to you.

`sc1` volumes could be considered as an alternative to archival or blob storage systems, such as `s3`, as the cost is broadly similar, but with the advantage that no special libraries or tools are needed to read and write data from them and, of course, with much lower latencies before the data can be read and used.

In use cases like Kafka, or log management, you might consider using `sc1` volumes for older data that you still need to keep in online storage, so it is available for immediate use, but where it is accessed less often so you want to optimize the cost of storage.

Networking

When running distributed systems, network performance can be a key factor on the overall observable performance of an application.

Architectural patterns that encourage building applications where communication between different components is primarily through the network (for example, SOA and microservices) lead to applications where intra-cluster networking can be a performance bottleneck. Clustered datastores also can place high demands on intra-cluster networking, especially during write operations and when rebalancing a cluster during scaling or maintenance operations.

Of course, network performance is also a factor to consider when running services that are exposed to the internet or other wide-area networks.

The latest generation of EC2 instance types benefit from a networking interface that AWS describes as enhanced networking. To benefit from this, you need to be running a relatively recent instance type (M5, C5, or R4) and have a special network driver installed for Amazon's Elastic Network Adapter. Luckily, if you are using an official AMI of any of the main Linux distributions, this should already be done for you.

You can check that you have the correct drivers installed with the `modinfo` command:

```
$ modinfo ena
filename:          /lib/modules/4.4.11-
23.53.amzn1.x86_64/kernel/drivers/amazon/net/ena/ena.ko
version:           0.6.6
license:           GPL
description:       Elastic Network Adapter (ENA)
author:            Amazon.com, Inc. or its affiliates
...
```

If the drivers for the **Elastic Network Interface** are not installed, you will see something like this:

```
$ modinfo ena
ERROR: modinfo: could not find module ena
```

The performance boost from enhanced networking doesn't cost anything extra to use, so it is something you should check is configured correctly whenever preparing for production. The only instances in common use that do not support enhanced networking are the t2 burstable instance types.

The network performance of EC2 instances is proportional to the instance size, with only the largest instance sizes of each instance types capable of the headline network throughputs of 10 or 20 GBps. Even when using the largest EC2 instance sizes, the headline network throughputs are only achievable when communicating to other instances within a cluster placement group.

A cluster placement group can be used to request that Amazon starts each of the instances you require together in a particular area in their data centers so the fastest speeds (and lowest latency) are available. To improve network performance, we can adjust two variables:

- **Increasing instance size**: This makes faster networking available to the instance, and also increases collocation so making localhost network calls between services more likely.
- **Adding your instance to a cluster placement group**: This ensures that your instances are hosted physically nearby, improving network performance.

Before taking decisions like this, you need to know that the network is really your performance bottleneck, because all of these choices make your cluster more at risk from underlying failures in AWS's infrastructure. So, unless you already know that your particular application will make particular demands on cluster networking, you shouldn't try to optimize for greater performance.

Security

Some of the key areas that impact security are show in this diagram:

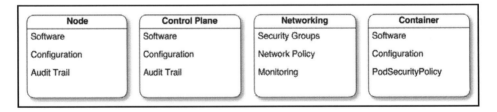

Securing the configuration and software that forms the infrastructure of your cluster is of vital importance, especially if you plan to expose the services you run on it to the internet.

You should consider that if you expose services to the public internet that have well known software vulnerabilities or configuration errors, it may only be a matter of hours before your services are detected by automated tools being used to scan for vulnerable systems.

It is important that you treat the security of your cluster as a moving target. This means that you, or a tool that you use, need to be aware of new software vulnerabilities and configuration vulnerabilities.

Vulnerabilities with the Kubernetes software, and with the underlying operating system software of your hosts, will be updated and patched by the Kubernetes community and your operating system vendor, simply requiring the operator to have a procedure to apply updates as they become available.

More critical is the configuration of your environment, as the responsibility for validating its security and correctness falls on your shoulders alone. As well as taking the time to validate and test the configuration, you should treat the security of your configuration as a moving target. You should ensure that you take the time to review changes and advice in the Kubernetes change log as you make updates.

Always be updating

A new minor version of Kubernetes is released approximately every three months. And the project can release patch-level updates to each released minor versions as often as once a week. The patch level updates will typically include fixes for more major bugs, and fixes for security issues. The Kubernetes community currently supports three minor versions at any one time, ending regular patch-level updates of the oldest supported version as each new minor version is released. This means that when you plan and build a cluster, you need to plan for two kinds of maintenance to the Kubernetes software:

- **Patch-level updates**: Up to several times a month:
  - These should maintain very close compatibility and mostly be trivial to perform.
  - They should be simple to perform with very little (or no) downtime.
- **Minor version upgrades**: Every 3 to 9 months:
  - You might need to make minor changes to the configuration of your cluster, when upgrading between minor versions.
  - Kubernetes does maintain good backwards compatibility, and has a strategy of deprecating config options before they are removed or changed. Just remember to take note of deprecation warnings in the change log and log output.

- If you are using third-party applications (or have written your own tools) that depend on beta or alpha APIs, you might need to update those tools before upgrading the cluster. Tools that only use the stable APIs should continue to work between minor version updates.
- You might need to think about the following:
  - A testing environment where you can apply updates to the Kubernetes software to validate any changes before you release them to your production environment.
  - Procedures or tools that will allow you to roll back any version upgrades, if you detect any errors.
  - Monitoring that allows you to determine that your cluster is functioning as expected.
- The procedures that you use to update the software on the machines that make up your cluster really depend on the tools that you are using.

There are two main strategies that you might take—upgrading in place, and an immutable image-based update strategy.

In-place updates

There are several tools that allow you to upgrade the underlying operating system on the nodes of your cluster. Tools such as `unattended-upgrades` for Debian-based systems or `yum-cron` for Red Hat-based systems allow you to install updated packages on your nodes without any operator input.

This, of course, can be somewhat risky in a production environment if a particular update causes the system to fail.

Typically, if you are managing a system with automatic updates, you would use the package manager to pin essential components, such as Kubernetes and **etcd**, to a particular version, and then handle upgrading these components in a more controlled way, perhaps with a configuration management tool, such as Puppet, Chef, or Ansible.

When upgrading packages like this in an automated way, a reboot of the system is required when certain components are updated. Tools such as the **KUbernetes REboot Daemon (Kured)**, (`https://github.com/weaveworks/kured`) can watch for a signal that a particular node requires a reboot and orchestrate rebooting nodes across the cluster in order to maintain uptime of the services running on the cluster. This is achieved by first signaling the Kubernetes Scheduler to re-schedule workloads to other nodes and then triggering a reboot.

There is also a new breed of operating systems, such as CoreOS' Container Linux or Google's Container-Optimized OS, that take a slightly different approach to updates. These new container-optimized Linux distributions don't provide a traditional package manager at all, instead requiring you to run everything not in the base system (like Kubernetes) as a container.

These systems handle updates of the base operating system much more like the firmware update systems found in consumer electronics. The base root filesystem in these operating systems is read-only and mounted from one of two special partitions. This allows the system to download a new operating system image to the unused partition in the background. When the system is ready to be upgraded, it is rebooted and the new image from the second partition is mounted as the root filesystem.

This has the advantage that if an upgrade fails or causes the system to become unstable, it is simple to roll back to the last version; indeed, this process can even become automated.

If you are using Container Linux, you can use the **Container Linux Update Operator** to orchestrate reboots due to OS updates (`https://github.com/coreos/container-linux-update-operator`). Using this tool, you can ensure that the workloads on your hosts are rescheduled before they are rebooted.

Immutable images

Whilst there are tools to help manage upgrading your hosts in place, there are some advantages to be had from embracing a strategy using immutable images.

Once you are managing the applications that run on your infrastructure with Kubernetes, the software that needs to be installed on your node becomes standardized. This means that it becomes much simpler to manage updating the configuration of your hosts as immutable images.

This could be attractive, as it allows you to manage building and deploying your node software in a similar way to building application containers with Docker.

Typically, if you take this approach, you will want to use a tool that simplifies building images in the AMI format and making them available for other tools to start new EC2 instances to replace those launched with a previous image. One such tool is packer.

Network security

When running Kubernetes on AWS, there are four different layers you will need to configure in order to correctly secure the traffic on your cluster.

Infra-node networking

In order for traffic to pass between pods and services running on your cluster, you will need to configure the AWS group(s) applied to your nodes to allow this traffic. If you are using an overlay network, this typically means allowing traffic on a particular port, as all communication is encapsulated to pass over a single port (typically as UDP packets). For example, the flannel overlay network is typically configured to communicate through UPD on port `7890`.

When using a native VPC networking solution, such as `amazon-vpc-cni-k8s`, it is typically necessary to allow all traffic to pass between the nodes. The `amazon-vpc-cni-k8s` plugin associates multiple pod IP addresses with a single Elastic Network Interface, so it is not typically possible to manage infra-node networking in a more granular way using security groups.

Node-master networking

In normal operations, the kubelet running on your nodes needs to connect to the Kubernetes API to discover the definitions of the pods it is expected to be running.

Typically, this means allowing TCP connections to be made on port `443` from your worker nodes to your control plane security group.

The control plane connects to the kubelet on an API exposed on port `10250`. This is needed for the `logs` and `exec` functionality.

External networking

Correctly understanding what traffic from outside your cluster is allowed to access your nodes is a critical part of keeping your cluster secure.

Recently, several researchers have discovered a significant number of otherwise secured clusters that allow unlimited access to the Kubernetes dashboard, and thus the cluster itself, to anyone accessing them on the internet.

Typically, in these cases, the cluster administrator had failed to properly configure the dashboard to authenticate users. But had they thought carefully about the services that were exposed to the wider internet, these breaches may have been avoided. Only exposing sensitive services like this to specific IP addresses or to users accessing your VPC through a VPN would have provided an additional layer of security.

When you do want to expose a service (or an ingress controller) to the wider internet, the Kubernetes Load Balancer service type will configure appropriate security groups for you (as well as provisioning an **Elastic Load Balancer** (**ELB**)).

Kubernetes infra-pod networking

Out of the box, Kubernetes doesn't provide any facilities for controlling the network access between pods running on your cluster. Any pod running on the cluster can connect to any other pod or service.

This might be reasonable for smaller deployments of fully-trusted applications. If you want to provide policies to restrict the connectivity between different applications running on your cluster, you will need to deploy a network plugin that will enforce Kubernetes networking policies, such as Calico, Romana, or WeaveNet.

Whist there is a large choice of network plugins that can be used to support the enforcement of the Kubernetes Network policy, if you have chosen to make use of AWS-supported native VPC networking, it is recommended to use Calico, as this configuration is supported by AWS. AWS provide example configuration to deploy Calico alongside the `amazon-vpc-cni-k8s` plugin in their GitHub repository: `https://github.com/aws/amazon-vpc-cni-k8s`.

The Kubernetes API provides the `NetworkPolicy` resource to provide policies to control the ingress and egress of traffic from pods. Each `NetworkPolicy` targets the pods that it will affect with a label selector and namespace. As the default is for pods to have no networking isolation, it can be useful if you wish to be strict to provide a default `NetworkPolicy` that will block traffic for pods that haven't yet been provided with a specific network policy.

 Check the Kubernetes documentation for some examples of default network policies to allow and deny all traffic by default at `https://kubernetes.io/docs/concepts/services-networking/network-policies/#default-policies`.

IAM roles

Kubernetes ships with some deep integrations with AWS. This means that Kubernetes can perform such tasks as provisioning EBS volumes and attaching them to the EC2 instances in your cluster, setting up ELB, and configuring security groups on your behalf.

In order for the Kubernetes to have the access it requires to perform these actions, you need to provide IAM credentials to allow the control plane and the nodes the required amount of access.

Typically, the most convenient way to do this is to attach an instance profile associated with a relevant IAM role to grant the Kubernetes processes running on the instance the required permissions. You saw an example of this in Chapter 3, *Reach for the Cloud*, when we launched a small cluster using `kubeadm`. When planning for a production cluster, there are a few more considerations you should plan for:

- *Are you running multiple clusters? Do you need cluster resources to be isolated?*
- *Do the applications running on your cluster also need to access resources within AWS that require authentication?*
- *Do the nodes in your cluster need to authenticate with the Kubernetes API using the AWS IAM Authenticator?* This will also apply if you are using Amazon EKS.

If you are running multiple clusters in your AWS account (for example, for production and staging or development environments), it is worth thinking about how you can tailor your IAM roles to prevent clusters from interfering with one another's resources.

In theory, a cluster shouldn't interfere with the resources created by another, but you might value the extra security that separate IAM roles for each environment can provide. Not sharing IAM roles between production and development or staging environments is good practice and can prevent configuration errors (or even bugs in Kubernetes) in one environment causing harm to resources associated with another cluster. Most resources that Kubernetes interacts with are tagged with a `kubernetes.io/cluster/<cluster name>` tag. With some of these resources, IAM offers the ability to restrict certain actions to resources matching that tag. Restricting delete actions in this way is one way to reduce the potential for harm.

When the applications running on your cluster need to access AWS resources, there are a number of ways to provide credentials to the AWS client libraries in order to authenticate correctly. You could supply credentials to your applications with secrets mounted as config files or as environment variables. But one of the most convenient ways to provide IAM credentials is to associate IAM roles to your pods using the same mechanism as instance profiles.

Tools such as `kube2iam` or `kiam` intercept calls made by the AWS client library to the metadata service and provide tokens depending on an annotation set on the pod. This allows IAM roles to be assigned as part of your normal deployment process.

kiam (`https://github.com/uswitch/kiam`) and **kube2iam** (`https://github.com/jtblin/kube2iam`) are two similar projects designed to provide IAM credentials to Kubernetes pods. Both projects run as an agent on each node, adding network routes to route traffic destined for the AWS metadata service. kiam additionally runs a central server component that is responsible for requesting tokens from the AWS API and maintains a cache of the credentials required for all running pods. This approach is noted to be more reliable in production clusters and reduces IAM the permissions required by the node agents.

Another advantage of using one of these tools is that it prevents the applications running on the cluster from using the permissions assigned to the underlying instance, reducing the risk that an application could errant or maliciously access resources providing control plane services.

Validation

When setting up a cluster, there are many different choices you might make to configure your cluster. It is important that you have some way to quickly validate that your cluster will operate correctly.

This is a problem that the Kubernetes community has solved in order to certify that different Kubernetes distributions are *conformant*. To gain a seal of approval that a particular Kubernetes distribution is conformant, it is necessary for a set of integration tests to be run against a cluster. These tests are useful for a vendor supplying a pre-packaged installation of Kubernetes to prove that their distribution functions correctly. It is also very useful for cluster operators to use to quickly validate that configuration changes of software updates leave your cluster in an operable state.

Kubernetes conformance testing is based on a number of specially automated tests from the Kubernetes code base. These tests are run against testing clusters as part of the end-to-end validation of the Kubernetes code base, and must pass before every change to the code base is merged in.

It certainly is possible to download the Kubernetes code base (and set up a Golang development environment) and configure it to run the conformance test directly. However, there is a tool called **Sonobuoy** that can automate this process for you.

 Sonobuoy makes it simple to run a set of Kubernetes conformance tests on your clusters in a simple and standardized manner. The simplest way to get started with Sonobuoy is to use the hosted browser-based service at `https://scanner.heptio.com/`. This service gives you a manifest to submit to your cluster and then displays the test results once the tests have finished running. If you want to run everything on your own cluster, you can install a command-line tool that will let you run tests and collect the results yourself by following the instructions at `https://github.com/heptio/sonobuoy`.

Kubernetes conformance testing is important because it exercises a wide range of Kubernetes features, giving you early warning of any misconfiguration before you have even deployed applications to your cluster that might exercise those features. It can be very helpful when making changes to the configuration of your cluster to have a warning if your changes might affect the functionality of the cluster.

Whilst Kubernetes conformance tests focus on testing the functionality of your cluster, security benchmarking checks your cluster's configuration against known unsafe configuration settings, ensuring that your cluster is configured to meet current security best practices.

The **Centre for Internet Security** publishes step-by-step checklists that you can manually follow to test your cluster against security best practices.

 You can download a copy of these benchmarks for free at `https://www.cisecurity.org/benchmark/kubernetes/`.

It can be useful to read and follow the advice in these checklists whist building your cluster, as it will help you to understand the reasons for a particular configuration value.

Once you have set up your cluster it can be useful to automatically validate your configuration as you update and make changes, to avoid your configuration accidentally drifting away from a secure configuration.

 `kube-bench` is a tool that provides an automated way to run the CIS benchmarks against your cluster: `https://github.com/aquasecurity/kube-bench`.

You might find it useful to also write your own integration tests that check that you can successfully deploy and operate some of your own applications. Tests like these can act as an important sanity check when rapidly developing the configuration for your cluster.

There are many tools that could be used to perform tests like these. I would recommend whatever test automation tool that the engineers in your organization are already comfortable with. You could use a tool specially designed for running automated tests, such as cucumber, but a simple shell script that deploys an application to your cluster and then checks that it is accessible is a great start too.

Observability

Observability is shown in the following diagram:

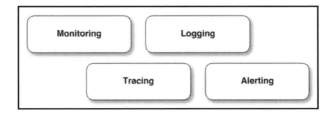

Being able to monitor and debug a cluster is one of the most important points to bear in mind when designing a cluster for production. Luckily, there are a number of solutions for managing logs and metrics that have very good support for Kubernetes.

Logging

Whenever you want to know what your applications are doing, the first thing most operators will think to do is to look at the logs generated by the application.

Logs are simple to understand, and they don't require any special tools to produce, as your application probably already supports some sort of the logging already.

Out of the box, Kubernetes allows you to view and tail the logs that your application is writing to standard out and standard errors. Using the `kubectl logs` command should be familiar to you if you have used the `docker logs` command on your own machine or on a server.

It is more convenient than logging into each node to view the logs generated by a particular container. As well as viewing the logs from a particular pod, `kubectl logs` can show the logs from all the pods matching a particular label expression.

If you need to search the logs generated by your application for a particular event, or if you need to see the logs generated at a particular time in the past, then you need to consider deploying a solution to aggregate and manage your logs.

The most widely used tool to implement this function is **Fluentd**. Fluentd is a very flexible tool that can be used to collect logs from a wide variety of sources and then push them to one or more destinations. If your organization already maintains or uses a third-party tool to aggregate application logs, you will almost certainly find a way to configure Fluentd to store the application logs from applications running on Kubernetes in your chosen tool. Members of the Fluentd team, and the wider community, maintain over 800 different plugins that support many different inputs, outputs, and filtering options.

As Fluentd is built upon the Ruby programming language, its plugins are distributed using the Rubygems package system. By convention, all Fluentd plugins have a name beginning with **fluent-plugin**, and all currently available plugins are listed here: `https://www.fluentd.org/plugins/all`. Because some of these plugins are maintained by the wider community, it is worth making some initial tests of a plugin you plan to use. The quality of plugins can be variable, depending on the stage of development a particular plugin is in and how often it is maintained. You can install and manage Fluentd plugins using the `gem install` command or control the exact versions of Fluentd plugins using the **bundler** tool. You can read more about installing plugins in your Fluentd installation here: `https://docs.fluentd.org/v1.0/articles/plugin-management`.

Monitoring

Looking at the log output of your application can be useful if you know there is an issue with an application and want to debug the cause. But it is much harder if you don't know where in your system a problem is occurring, or if you simply want to assess the health of a system.

Your logs are very flexible because your applications can write any information in an unstructured way to a logging endpoint. This in a large system can become quite overwhelming, and the amount of effort required to filter and analyze this output can become complex.

Monitoring or metrics collection takes a different approach. By defining measurements that reflect the performance and operation of your system, of Kubernetes, and your infrastructure, you can much more quickly answer questions about the health and performance of your system.

Collected metrics are also one of the most useful sources for automated alerting systems. They can warn members of your organization about abnormal behavior in your applications or infrastructure.

There are a number of commercial and open source tools that can be used to collect metrics and create alerts. The decision you take will most likely be influenced by your organization and the requirements you have.

As I have already said, trying to introduce too many new tools or processes to your organization at once can risk your success. In many cases, many monitoring tools already support integration with Kubernetes. If this is the case, it may be prudent to consider continuing to use the existing tools your organization is used to.

Whichever tools you choose to record metrics from your applications and from the cluster and the underlying infrastructure, you should think carefully about how to make it simple for members of your organization who are responsible for developing and deploying applications to surface their metrics. As part of planning your cluster, try writing the documentation for the procedure to expose metrics that should be followed by a developer deploying a new application to your cluster. You should aim to keep this process as simple as possible. If you need to automate steps of the process and provide default configuration values, you should do so in order to make the process simple. If the process of exporting new metrics from your applications is complex or requires lots of manual steps, then it becomes less likely that your organization's applications will expose them.

If the process is simple and friction-free, it becomes much simpler to instill a culture of monitoring by default. If, for example, you choose to use Prometheus, you might document the process like this:

- * expose an endpoint `/metrics` on port `9102`
- Add the annotation `"prometheus.io/scrape": true` to your pod

In this example, by configuring Prometheus with sensible defaults, exposing metrics from a pod becomes quick and simple for a developer. It is possible to expose more complex configuration for the way that Prometheus will scrape metrics, but by using well-known default values, it makes the setup process simpler and makes it simpler to include a standard Prometheus library in the application. Whatever system you choose to use to collect metrics, try to follow these principles wherever possible.

Collecting metrics directly from application pods and the infrastructure provides deep and rich information about how your application is behaving. This information is very useful when you need to know specifics about the application and can be very useful for pre-empting issues. For example, metrics about disk usage could be used to provide alerts that warn operators about a state that could lead to an application failure if not addressed.

Blackbox monitoring

Whilst application-specific metrics provide deep insight that is useful for root cause analysis and pre-emptive alerting, Blackbox monitoring takes the opposite approach. By treating the application as a sealed entity, and exercising user-facing endpoints, you can surface the symptoms of a badly performing application. Blackbox monitoring can be implemented by using a tool such as the Prometheus Blackbox exporter. But another common pattern is to use a commercial service. The main advantage of this is that they typically allow you to probe applications from a number of locations, perhaps globally, truly exercising the full stack of infrastructure between your users and your applications.

Alerting

Recording metrics about the state of the systems you are running on Kubernetes is the first stage of making your systems simple to observe. Once you have collected your metrics there are several ways to make the data you collect simple to act upon.

Most metrics collection tools offer some way to build graphs and dashboards for the metrics that are important to different members of your organization. For example, many users of Prometheus use Grafana to build dashboards to expose important metrics.

Whilst a dashboard is a good way to get an idea of how a particular system or business process is performing, there are aspects of your system that need a more proactive approach.

Any metrics-gathering system worth its salt will offer a way to emit alerts to members of your organization. However, when you gather metrics and whatever system you use to send alerts to your team, there are a few principles you should consider:

- **Alerts should be actionable**: When promoting a metric from a graph or gauge on a dashboard to an alert, make sure you only send alerts for states that need immediate human intervention, not merely warnings or information. Warnings or informational alerts belong on your dashboards, not on your pager.
- **Alerts should be used sparingly**: Alerts interrupt people from whatever they are doing at that moment: working, resting, or, worst of all, sleeping. If a person receives too many alerts they can be a cause of stress, and quickly become less effective as alert fatigue sets in and they lose their attention-grabbing power. When designing an alerting mechanism, you should make provision to record how often members of your organization are interrupted by your alerting.

Alerts should be directed—you should think about who should be responsible for a particular alert and direct it appropriately. Alerts can be directed to a number of systems, such as bug trackers, emails, chat systems, and even pager applications. It is important that the person who receives the most mission-critical alerts from your organization is in a position to take ownership and manage a response. Less important alerts might be assigned to a team or group in a bug tracking tool. If your organization makes use of a chat system, such as Slack, HipChat, or IRC, you might want to direct alerts for a particular application to a channel or room used by the team that develops or is responsible for the operation of that application. Just remember to ensure that volumes are kept to an acceptable level or your alerts will quickly come to be ignored by the people who need to know about them.

Tracing

Tracing is the youngest member of the observability family and is thus often the last one an organization will choose to implement. The idea of a tracing system is to measure the time a single request takes to pass through your applications.

This might not expose any more interesting information than well-configured metrics for a monolithic application. But for larger-scale systems with a distributed, or *microservices* architecture, where a single request can pass through tens or even hundreds of separate processes, tracing can help to pinpoint exactly when and where performance issues are occurring.

When implementing a system to collect tracing information from your applications, you have a number of options.

AWS's built-in solution for tracing includes X-Ray ships with support for Java, Go Node.js, Python, Ruby, and .NET applications. For these technologies, adding distributed tracing to your applications is simply a question of adding a library to your applications and configuring it correctly. https://aws.amazon.com/xray/.

Competing with AWS's solution is a number of tools that are designed to work together under the OpenTracing banner.

OpenTracing provides client libraries for nine languages that are compatible with nine different open source and commercial tools designed to collect trace data. Because of the open nature of OpenTracing, several application frameworks, and infrastructure components, are choosing to add support for its trace format. You can find out more about OpenTracing at http://opentracing.io.

Summary

This chapter has, hopefully, given you an idea of the myriad different options and decisions you can make when deciding to run Kubernetes in a production environment. Don't let the depth and breadth of the options and choices to make put you off, as Kubernetes is remarkably easy to get started with, especially on AWS.

In the next chapter, we will move to the practical work of getting a cluster set up and ready for work. We won't be able to cover all of the options, let alone all of the add-ons and additional tools that the community around Kubernetes has produced, but we will provide a stable starting point from which you can begin to implement your own plans.

Hopefully, this chapter will serve as a guide for you and your team to discuss and plan a cluster that meets the needs of your organization. You can then start to implement the features and functionality that you may have identified while reading this chapter.

If there is one single thing to remember when launching your own cluster: keep it simple, silly. Kubernetes makes it simple to add new tools to your arsenal whenever you need, so don't over-complicate or over-engineer too fast. Start with the simplest setup that can possibly work, even if you think you need to add complexity later; often, you will discover that the simple solution works just fine.

Take advantage of the fact that Kubernetes itself will allow you to rapidly evolve your infrastructure, and start small and add features and tools to your system when you need them, and not before!

A Production-Ready Cluster

7

In the last chapter, we spent some time thinking about a framework for planning a Kubernetes cluster. Hopefully, it should be clear to you that, when building a cluster, there are lots of decisions to make based on the requirements of the systems you are running.

In this chapter, we will take a much more practical approach to this problem. Instead of trying to cover the myriad options available to us, I will start by making some choices, and then we will build a fully functional cluster that will serve as a base configuration to build upon for many different use cases.

In this chapter, we will cover the following topics:

- Terraform
- Preparing node images and a node group
- Provisioning add-ons

Building a cluster

The information contained within this chapter is just one possible way that you could approach building and managing a cluster. When building a Kubernetes cluster, there are many choices to be made, and almost as many tools that could be chosen. For the purposes of this chapter, I have chosen to use tools that make it simple to illustrate the process of building a cluster. If you or your team has a preference for using different tools, then the concepts and architecture outlined in this chapter will transfer quite easily to other tools.

In this chapter, we are going to launch our cluster in a way that will make it more suitable for production workloads. Much of what we do here will be familiar to you from Chapter 3, *Reach for the Cloud*, but we are going to build on the process we outlined there in two key ways. Firstly, when building infrastructure that you depend on, it is very important that you are able to quickly roll out a new instance of your infrastructure in a manner that is repeatable. We want to be able to do this because it makes it simple to test changes that we want to make to our infrastructure in a risk-free way. By automating the provisioning of a Kubernetes cluster, we enable the patterns of immutable infrastructure that we previously discussed. Instead of risking upgrading or changing our production infrastructure, we can quickly provision a replacement cluster that we can then test before moving our workloads to the new cluster.

In order to achieve this, we are going to use the Terraform infrastructure provisioning tool to interact with AWS. Terraform allows us to define our infrastructure as code using a programming language of sorts. By defining our infrastructure as code, we are able to use tools such as version control and follow other software development practices to manage the evolution of our infrastructure.

In this chapter, we are about to make a lot of decisions about what a Kubernetes cluster running on AWS should look like and how it should be managed. For the purposes of this chapter and the example that we will be dealing with, I have the following requirements in mind.

- **Illustrative**: We will see what a Kubernetes cluster that meets the requirements of an average production use case might look like. This cluster reflects the decisions that I have personally taken when designing Kubernetes clusters that are intended for real production use. In order to make this chapter as clear and easy to understand as I can, I have tried to keep the cluster and its configuration as simple as possible.
- **Flexible**: We will create something that you can treat as a template and add to or alter to meet your needs.
- **Extendable**: Whenever you are designing a Kubernetes cluster (or indeed any infrastructure), you should think about the decisions that you make now that might prevent you from extending or expanding that infrastructure later.

Clearly, when you are building your own cluster, you should have a much more concrete idea of your requirements so that you will be able to tailor your cluster to your own needs. The cluster we will build here will be a great starting point for any production-ready system that you can then customize and add to as required.

Much of the configuration in this chapter has been shortened. You can check out the full configuration used in this chapter at `https://github.com/PacktPublishing/Kubernetes-on-AWS/tree/master/chapter07`.

Getting started with Terraform

Terraform is a command-line tool that you can run on your workstation to make changes to your infrastructure. Terraform is a single binary that just needs to be installed onto your path.

You can download Terraform from `https://www.terraform.io/downloads.html` for six different operating systems, including macOS, Windows, and Linux. Download the ZIP file for your operating system, extract it, and then copy the Terraform binary to a location on your path.

Terraform uses files with the `.tf` extension to describe your infrastructure. Because Terraform supports the management of resources on many different cloud platforms, it can contain the concepts of the relevant providers, which are loaded as required to support the different APIs exposed by the different cloud providers.

First, let's configure the AWS Terraform provider in order to be ready to build a Kubernetes cluster. Create a new directory to hold the Terraform configuration for your Kubernetes cluster, and then create a file where we will configure the AWS provider, as shown in the following code:

```
aws.tf
provider "aws" {
  version = "~> 1.0"

  region = "us-west-2"
}
```

Save the file, and then run the following:

```
terraform.init
Initializing provider plugins...
- Checking for available provider plugins on
https://releases.hashicorp.com...
- Downloading plugin for provider "aws" (1.33.0)...
Terraform has been successfully initialized!
```

When you use a supported provider, Terraform can discover and download the required plugin for you. Note that we have already configured the provider with an AWS region of `us-west-2`, as this is the region where we will be launching our cluster in this example.

In order for Terraform to communicate with the AWS API, you will need to provide the AWS provider with some credentials. We learned how to obtain credentials in `Chapter 3`, *Reach for the Cloud*. If you followed the advice in `Chapter 3`, *Reach for the Cloud*, and set your credentials up with the `aws configure` command, then Terraform will read your default credentials from your local config file.

Alternatively, Terraform can read AWS credentials from the `AWS_ACCESS_KEY_ID` and `AWS_SECRET_ACCESS_KEY` environment variables, or, if you are running Terraform on an EC2 instance, it can use the credentials provided by an EC2 instance role.

It is also possible to statically configure the credentials by adding an `access_key` and `secret_key` parameter inline in the AWS provider block, but I wouldn't really recommend this practice as it makes it much harder to check your configuration into a version control system.

By default, Terraform uses a local file called `terraform.tfstate` to keep track of the state of your infrastructure. This is so that it can keep track of the changes you have made to the configuration since you last ran Terraform.

If you are going to be the only person managing your infrastructure, then this might be acceptable, but you would need to securely back up the state file. It should be considered sensitive, and Terraform won't function correctly if you lose it.

If you are using AWS, I would recommend using S3 as a backend. You can read about how to set this up in the Terraform documentation at `https://www.terraform.io/docs/backends/types/s3.html`. If configured correctly, S3 storage is highly secure, and if you are working on a team, then you can utilize a DynamoDB table as a lock to ensure that multiple instances of Terraform are not running at the same time. If you want to make use of this, set the configuration in the `backend.tf` file, otherwise delete that file.

Variables

Terraform allows us to define variables in order to make our configuration more reusable. This is particularly useful if you later want to use your configuration as a module in order to define multiple clusters. We won't cover that in this chapter, but we can follow best practices and define some key variables to allow you to simply shape the cluster to meet your needs.

It is standard to create a `variables.tf` file to include all of the variables in your project. This is helpful because it acts as high-level documentation about how your configuration can be controlled.

As you can see, between choosing descriptive names for my variables and adding the optional description field, the whole file is quite self-explanatory. Because I have provided defaults for each variable, we can run Terraform without passing any values for these variables, as shown in the following code:

```
variables.tf
variable "cluster_name" {
  default = "lovelace"
}

variable "vpc_cidr" {
  default     = "10.1.0.0/16"
  description = "The CIDR of the VPC created for this cluster"
}

variable "availability_zones" {
  default     = ["us-west-2a","us-west-2b"]
  description = "The availability zones to run the cluster in"
}

variable "k8s_version" {
  default     = "1.10"
  description = "The version of Kubernetes to use"
}
```

Networking

We will start by creating a config file to describe the network setup for our Kubernetes cluster. You might recognize the design of this network, as it is quite similar the one we manually created in Chapter 3, *Reach for the Cloud*, but with a few additions to make it more suitable for a production setup.

Terraform configuration files can be documented with comments, and to better illustrate this configuration, I have provided some commentary in the form of comments. You will notice that they are surrounded by /* and */.

In order to support high availability, we are going to create subnets for more than one availability zone, as shown in the following code. Here, we are using two, but if you wanted even greater resiliency, you can easily add another availability zone to the `availability_zones` variable:

```
networking.tf
/*  Set up a VPC for our cluster.
*/resource "aws_vpc" "k8s" {
  cidr_block          = "${var.vpc_cidr}"
  enable_dns_hostnames = true

  tags = "${
    map(
      "Name", "${var.cluster_name}",
      "kubernetes.io/cluster/${var.cluster_name}", "shared",
    )
  }"
}

/*  In order for our instances to connect to the internet
   we provision an internet gateway.*/
resource "aws_internet_gateway" "gateway" {
  vpc_id = "${aws_vpc.k8s.id}"

  tags {
    Name = "${var.cluster_name}"
  }
}

/*  For instances without a Public IP address we will route traffic
   through a NAT Gateway. Setup an Elastic IP and attach it.

   We are only setting up a single NAT gateway, for simplicity.
   If the availability is important you might add another in a
   second availability zone.
*/
resource "aws_eip" "nat" {
  vpc        = true
  depends_on = ["aws_internet_gateway.gateway"]
}

resource "aws_nat_gateway" "nat_gateway" {
```

```
    allocation_id = "${aws_eip.nat.id}"
    subnet_id     = "${aws_subnet.public.*.id[0]}"
}
```

We are going to provision two subnets for each of the availability zones we are using for our cluster. A public subnet which have a direct route to the internet where Kubernetes will provision load balancers that are accessible to the internet. And a private subnet that will be used by Kubernetes to assign IP addresses to pods.

Because the address space available in the private subnets will be the limiting factor on the number of pods that Kubernetes will be able to launch, we provision a large address range with 16382 available IP addresses. This should allow our cluster some room for expansion.

If you are only planning to run internal services that are not be accessible to the internet, then you might be able to skip the public subnets. You can find the full `networking.tf` file in the example files for this chapter.

Plan and apply

Terraform allows us to incrementally build our infrastructure by adding to and changing the code that defines it. Then if you wish, as you go through this chapter, you can build up your configuration piece by piece, or you can use Terraform to build your whole cluster in one go.

Whenever you use Terraform to make a change to your infrastructure, it first produces a plan of the changes that it is going to make, and then it applies this plan. This two-stage operation is ideal when modifying production infrastructure as it gives you the opportunity to review the changes that will actually be applied to your cluster before they are made.

Once you have saved your networking configuration to a file, we can follow a few steps to safely provision our infrastructure.

We can check for syntax errors in the configuration by running the following command:

```
terraform validate
```

If your configuration is good, then there will be no output, but if there are syntax errors with your file(s), you should see an error message explaining the issue. For example, a missing closing brace might cause an error such as `Error parsing networking.tf: object expected closing RBRACE got: EOF`.

Once you have ensured that your files are correctly formatted for Terraform, you can create a plan for the changes to your infrastructure using the following command:

```
terraform plan -out k8s.plan
```

This command will output a summary of the changes that will be made to your infrastructure if this plan is run. The `-out` flag is optional, but it is a good idea because it allows us to apply exactly these changes later on. If you were paying attention to the output when you ran the Terraform plan, then you should have seen a message like:

```
To perform exactly these actions, run the following command to apply:
terraform apply "k8s.plan"
```

When you run `terraform apply` with a precomputed plan, it will make the changes that were outlined when the plan was generated. You could also run `terraform plan` command without pregenerating a plan, but in this case, it will still plan the changes and then prompt you before applying them.

Terraform computes the dependencies between the different resources in your infrastructure—for example, it ensures that the VPC is created before the route tables and other resources are created. Some resources can take a few seconds to create, but Terraform will wait until they are available before moving on to create dependent resources.

If you want to remove a resource that Terraform has created in your AWS account, you can just delete the definition from the relevant `.tf` file and then plan and apply your changes. When you are testing a Terraform configuration, it can be useful to remove all of the resources created by a particular configuration in order to test provisioning your infrastructure from scratch. If you need to do this, the `terraform destroy` command is very useful; it will remove all of the resources that are defined in your Terraform files from your infrastructure. However, be aware that this could cause essential resources to be terminated and removed, and so you shouldn't use this method on a running production system. Before any resources are removed, Terraform will list them and then ask you whether you want to remove them.

Control Plane

In order to provide a resilient and reliable Kubernetes Control Plane for our cluster, we are going to make our first big departure from the simple cluster that we built in `Chapter 3, Reach for the Cloud`.

As we learned in `Chapter 1`, *Google's Infrastructure for the Rest of Us*, the key components of the Kubernetes Control Plane are the backing etcd store, the API server, the scheduler, and the controller manager. If we want to build and manage a resilient control plane, we need to manage running these components across multiple instances, ideally spread across several availability zones.

Because the API server is stateless, and the scheduler and controller manager have built-in leader election facilities, it is relatively simple to run multiple instances on AWS, for example, by using an autoscaling group.

Running production-grade etcd is slightly trickier because etcd should be carefully managed when adding or removing nodes to avoid data loss and downtime. Successfully running an etcd cluster is quite a difficult task on AWS, and requires either manual operation or complex automation.

Luckily for us, AWS has developed a service that removes nearly all of the operational complexity involved in provisioning the Kubernetes Control Plane—**Amazon EKS**, or to use the full name, the Amazon Elastic Container Service for Kubernetes.

With EKS, AWS will manage and run the components that make up the Kubernetes Control Plane on your behalf across multiple availability zones, thus avoiding any single points of failure. With EKS, you no longer have to worry about performing or automating the operational tasks required for running a stable etcd cluster.

We should bear in mind that, with EKS, a key part of the infrastructure of our cluster is now managed by a third party. You should be comfortable with the fact that AWS can do a better job than your own team of providing a resilient control plane. This doesn't preclude you from designing your cluster to be somewhat resistant to the failure of the control plane—for example, if the kubelet cannot connect to the control plane, then the running containers will remain running until the control plane becomes available again. You should make sure that any additional components you add to your cluster can cope with temporary downtime in a similar fashion.

EKS reduces the amount of effort required to manage the most complex parts of Kubernetes (the control plane), thereby reducing the time (and money) required to design your cluster, and to maintain it. Moreover, for even a modestly sized cluster, the cost of the EKS service is significantly lower than the equivalent cost of running your own control plane across multiple EC2 instances.

In order for the Kubernetes Control Plane to manage resources in your AWS account, you need to provide EKS with an IAM role that will be assumed by EKS itself.

EKS creates network interfaces within your VPC to allow the Kubernetes Control Plane to communicate with the kubelet in order to provide services such as **log streaming** and **exec**. To control this communication, we need to supply EKS with a security group when it is launched. You can find the full Terraform configuration used to provision the control plane in `control_plane.tf` in the example files for this chapter.

We can use the Terraform resource for the EKS cluster to query it in order to fetch the endpoint for the Kubernetes API and the certificate authority that is used to access it.

This information, combined with Terraform's templating facilities, allows us to generate a `kubeconfig` file with the information required to connect to the Kubernetes API provided by EKS. We can use this later to provision add-on components.

If you want, you could also use this file to connect to the cluster manually with kubectl, either by copying the file to the default location at `~/.kube/config` or by passing its location to kubectl with the `--kubeconfig` flag or the `KUBECONFIG` environment variable, as shown in the following code:

The `KUBECONFIG` environment variable can be useful if you are managing multiple clusters, as you can easily load multiple configs by separating their paths; for example:
`export KUBECONFIG=$HOME/.kube/config:/path/to/other/conf.`

kubeconfig.tpl
```
apiVersion: v1
kind: Config
clusters:
- name: ${cluster_name}
  cluster:
    certificate-authority-data: ${ca_data}
    server: ${endpoint}
users:
- name: ${cluster_name}
  user:
    exec:
      apiVersion: client.authentication.k8s.io/v1alpha1
      command: aws-iam-authenticator
      args:
      - "token"
      - "-i"
      - "${cluster_name}"
contexts:
```

```
- name: ${cluster_name}
  context:
    cluster: ${cluster_name}
    user: ${cluster_name}
current-context: ${cluster_name}
```

Preparing node images

As we did in Chapter 3, *Reach for the Cloud*, we will now be preparing an AMI for the worker nodes in our cluster. However, we will improve this process by automating it with **Packer**. Packer is a tool that makes it simple to build machine images on AWS (and other platforms).

Installing Packer

Just like Terraform, Packer is distributed as a single binary that just needs to be copied to a location on your path. You can find detailed installation instructions on the Packer website at https://www.packer.io/intro/getting-started/install.html.

 Once you have installed Packer, you can run packer version to check that you have correctly copied it into to your path.

Packer configuration

Packer is configured with a JSON-formatted configuration file, that you can see at ami/node.json.

There are three parts to the example configuration here. The first is a list of variables. Here, we are using variables to store the version numbers of the important software that we are going to install in our image. This will make it simple to build and test images with updated versions of the Kubernetes software when it becomes available in the future.

The second part of the configuration configures the builder. Packer allows us to choose to build our image with one or more builders that support building images for different cloud providers. Since we want to build an image to use on AWS, we are using the `amazon-ebs` builder, which creates an image by launching a temporary EC2 instance and then creating an AMI from the contents of its root EBS volume (just like the manual procedure we followed in `Chapter 3`, *Reach for the Cloud*). This builder configuration allows us to choose the base image that our machine will be based on; here, we are using an official Ubuntu server image, a trusted source. The `ami-name` field in the builder configuration defines the name that the outputted image will be given. We have included the version of the Kubernetes software used and a timestamp to ensure that this image name is unique. Having a unique image name lets us define precisely which image to use when we deploy servers using it.

Finally, we configure a provisioner to install the software that our image will require. Packer supports many different provisioners that can install software, including full configuration-management systems such as Chef or Ansible. To keep this example simple, we will automate the installation of the software that we need by using a shell script. Packer will upload the configured script to the builder instance and then execute it via SSH.

We are just using a simple shell script, but if your organization already has a configuration-management tool in use, then you might prefer to use that to install the software that your image needs, especially as it makes it simple to include your organization's base configuration.

In this script, we are installing the software and configuration that our worker nodes will need to join an EKS cluster and function correctly, as shown in the following list. In a real deployment, there may be other tools and configurations that you wish to add in addition to these.

- **Docker**: Docker is currently the best tested and most common container runtime to use with Kubernetes
- **kubelet**: The Kubernetes node agent
- **ekstrap**: Configures the kubelet to connect to the EKS cluster endpoint
- **aws-iam-authenticator**: Allows the node to authenticate with the EKS cluster using the node's IAM credentials

We install these elements using the following code:

install.sh
```
        #!/bin/bash
        set -euxo pipefail
...
        # Install aws-iam-authenticator
```

```
curl -Lo /usr/local/bin/heptio-authenticator-aws
https://github.com/kubernetes-sigs/aws-iam-authenticator/releases/download/
v0.3.0/heptio-authenticator-aws_0.3.0_linux_amd64
chmod +x /usr/local/bin/heptio-authenticator-aws

apt-get install -y \
  docker-ce=$DOCKER_VERSION* \
  kubelet=$K8S_VERSION* \
  ekstrap=$EKSTRAP_VERSION*
# Cleanup
apt-get clean
rm -rf /tmp/*
   # Cleanup
   apt-get clean
   rm -rf /tmp/*
```

Once you have prepared the configuration for Packer, you can use the `packer build` command to build the AMI in your AWS account, as shown in the following code. This will start a temporary EC2 instance. Save the new AMI into your account and clean up the temporary instance:

packer build node.json

> If your organization uses a continuous integration service, you might want to configure it to build your node image on a regular schedule in order to pick up security updates to the base operating system.

Node group

Now that we have prepared an image for the worker nodes in our cluster, we can set up an autoscaling group to manage the launching of the EC2 instances that will form our cluster.

EKS doesn't tie us to managing our nodes in any particular way, so autoscaling groups are not the only option for managing the nodes in our cluster, but using them is one of the simplest ways of managing multiple worker instances in our cluster.

If you wanted to use multiple instance types in your cluster, you could repeat the launch configuration and autoscaling group configuration for each instance type that you wanted to use. In this configuration, we are launching c5.large instances on demand, but you should refer back to Chapter 6, *Planning for Production*, for more information about choosing appropriate instance sizes for your cluster.

The first part of the configuration sets up an IAM role for our instances to use. This is simple because AWS provides managed policies that have the permissions required by Kubernetes. The AmazonEKSWorkerNodePolicy code phrase allows the kubelet to query information about EC2 instances, attached volumes, and network settings, and to query information about EKS clusters. The AmazonEKS_CNI_Policy provides the permissions required by the vpc-cni-k8s network plugin to attach network interfaces to the instance and assign new IP addresses to those interfaces. The AmazonEC2ContainerRegistryReadOnly policy allows the instance to pull Docker images from the AWS Elastic Container Registry (you can read more about using this in Chapter 10, *Managing Container Images*). We will also manually specify a policy that will allow the kube2iam tool to assume roles in order to provide credentials to applications running on the cluster, as shown in the following code:

```
nodes.tf
/*
   IAM policy for nodes
*/
data "aws_iam_policy_document" "node" {
  statement {
    actions = ["sts:AssumeRole"]

    principals {
      type        = "Service"
      identifiers = ["ec2.amazonaws.com"]
    }
  }
}
...


resource "aws_iam_instance_profile" "node" {
  name = "${aws_iam_role.node.name}"
  role = "${aws_iam_role.node.name}"
}
```

Before our worker nodes can register themselves with the Kubernetes API server, they need to have the correct permissions to do so. In EKS, the mapping between IAM roles and users is configured by submitting a config map to the cluster.

 You can read more about how to map IAM users and roles to Kubernetes permissions in the EKS documentation at https://docs.aws.amazon.com/eks/latest/userguide/add-user-role.html.

Terraform will use the `kubeconfig` file that we produced while setting up the control plane in order to submit this configuration to the cluster using `kubectl` via the local-exec provisioner, as shown in the following `nodes.tf` continued code:

```
/*
  This config map configures which IAM roles should be trusted by
Kubernetes
*/

resource "local_file" "aws_auth" {
  content = <<YAML
apiVersion: v1
kind: ConfigMap
metadata:
  name: aws-auth
  namespace: kube-system
data:
  mapRoles: |
    - rolearn: ${aws_iam_role.node.arn}
      username: system:node:{{EC2PrivateDNSName}}
      groups:
        - system:bootstrappers
        - system:nodes
YAML
  filename = "${path.module}/aws-auth-cm.yaml"
  depends_on = ["local_file.kubeconfig"]

  provisioner "local-exec" {
    command = "kubectl --kubeconfig=${local_file.kubeconfig.filename} apply
-f ${path.module}/aws-auth-cm.yaml"
  }
}
```

Next, we need to prepare security groups to control the network traffic to and from our nodes.

We will set up a number of rules to allow the following communication flows that are required for our cluster to function correctly:

- Nodes need to communicate with each other for intracluster pod and service communication.
- The Kubelet running on the nodes needs to connect to the Kubernetes API server in order to read and update information about the state of the cluster.
- The control plane needs to connect to the Kubelet API on port `10250`; this is used for functionalities such as `kubectl exec` and `kubectl logs`.

- In order to use the proxy functionality of the API to proxy traffic to pods and services, the control plane needs to connect to pods that are running in the cluster. In this example, we are opening all of the ports, but if, for example, you only open unprivileged ports on your pods, then you would only need to allow traffic to ports above 1024.

We set these rules up using the following code. The code for nodes.tf is continued:

```
resource "aws_security_group" "nodes" {
  name        = "${var.cluster_name}-nodes"
  description = "Security group for all nodes in the cluster"
  vpc_id      = "${aws_vpc.k8s.id}"

  egress {
    from_port   = 0
    to_port     = 0
    protocol    = "-1"
    cidr_blocks = ["0.0.0.0/0"]
  }

...
resource "aws_security_group_rule" "nodes-control_plane-proxy" {
  description              = "API (proxy) communication to pods"
  from_port                = 0
  to_port                  = 65535
  protocol                 = "tcp"
  security_group_id        = "${aws_security_group.nodes.id}"
  source_security_group_id = \
                             "${aws_security_group.control_plane.id}"
  type                     = "ingress"
}
```

Now that we have prepared the infrastructure to run our nodes, we can prepare a launch configuration and assign it to an autoscaling group to actually launch our nodes, as shown in the following code.

Clearly, the instance type and disk size I have chosen here might not suit your cluster, so you will want to refer back to the information in Chapter 6, *Planning for Production*, when choosing an instance size for your cluster. The disk size required will be largely dependent on the average image size of your applications. The code for nodes.tf is continued:

```
data "aws_ami" "eks-worker" {
  filter {
    name   = "name"
    values = ["eks-worker-${var.k8s_version}*"]
  }
```

```
  most_recent = true
  owners      = ["self"]
}

...

resource "aws_autoscaling_group" "node" {
launch_configuration = "${aws_launch_configuration.node.id}"
max_size             = 2
min_size             = 10
name                 = "eks-node-${var.cluster_name}"
vpc_zone_identifier  = ["${aws_subnet.private.*.id}"]

tag {
  key               = "Name"
  value             = "eks-node-${var.cluster_name}"
  propagate_at_launch = true
}

tag {
  key               = "kubernetes.io/cluster/${var.cluster_name}"
  value             = "owned"
  propagate_at_launch = true
}
}
```

The `kubernetes.io/cluster/<node name>` tag is used by the `ekstrap` tool to discover the EKS endpoint in order to register the node with the cluster and by the `kubelet` to verify that it has connected to the correct cluster.

Provisioning add-ons

Much of the power of Kubernetes comes from the fact that it is easy to extend by adding additional services to provide additional functionality.

We are going to look at an example of this by deploying `kube2iam`. This is a daemon that runs on every node in our cluster and intercepts calls to the AWS metadata service that are made by processes running in our pods.

A simple way to provision a service like this is by using a DaemonSet to run a pod on every node in the cluster, as shown in the following code. This approach is already used in our cluster to deploy the `aws-vpc-cni` networking plugin to every node and to run `kube-proxy`, the Kubernetes component that runs on every node and that is responsible for routing traffic that is destined for service IPs to the underlying pods:

kube2iam.yaml
```
---
apiVersion: v1
kind: ServiceAccount
metadata:
  name: kube2iam
  namespace: kube-system
---
apiVersion: v1
kind: List
items:
...
```
                                                                    kube2iam.tf
```
resource "null_resource" "kube2iam" {
  triggers = {
    manifest_sha1 = "${sha1(file("${path.module}/kube2iam.yaml"))}"
  }

  provisioner "local-exec" {
    command = " kubectl --kubeconfig=${local_file.kubeconfig.filename}
apply -f
${path.module}/kube2iam.yaml"
  }
}
```

Managing change

Managing your Kubernetes clusters with a tool like Terraform offers a lot of advantages over the manual approach that we explored in Chapter 3, *Reach for the Cloud*. Being able to quickly and easily repeat the process of provisioning a cluster is very useful when you want to test changes to your configuration, or even when you come to upgrade the version of Kubernetes that your cluster is running.

The other key advantage of defining your infrastructure as code, is that you can use a version control tool to keep track of the changes that you make to your infrastructure over time. One of the key advantages to this is that every time you make a change, you can leave a commit message. Decisions that you make now might seem obvious, but having a record of why you chose to do something a certain way will certainly help you and others who have to work with your configuration in the future, especially as those others may not have the same context that you had when you made your changes.

A lot has been written about writing good commit messages by many software engineers. The best piece of advice is to make sure that you include as much information as is required to explain why your change was needed. Your future self will thank you if you have to return to the configuration months later.

Consider this commit message:

```
Update K8s Node Security Groups

Open port 80 on the Node Security Group
```

Also consider this commit message:

```
Allow deveopers to access the guestbook app

The guestbook is served from port 80. We are allowing the control plane
access to this port on the Node security groups, so developers can test the
application using kubectl proxy.

Once the application is in production and we provision a LoadBalancer, we
can remove these rules.
```

The first commit message is bad because it just explains what you did, and that should be obvious just by looking at how the configuration changed. The second message gives a lot more information. Importantly, the second message explains why the change needed to be made and gives some information that will be useful for anyone making changes to the cluster in the future. Without this important context, you might wonder why port 80 was opened and worry about what might happen if you changed that information.

Operating a Kubernetes cluster in a production setting is not just about how you launch the cluster on day one; it's about making sure that you can update and extend the cluster over time to continue to meet the requirements of your organization.

Summary

The cluster that we have built in this chapter is still quite simple, and really reflects a starting point that we can build upon in the following chapters. However, it does meet the following essential requirements for production readiness:

- **Reliability**: By using EKS, we have provisioned a reliable control plane that we can depend upon to manage our cluster.
- **Scalability**: By operating our nodes via an autoscaling group, we can make it simple to add extra capacity to our cluster in seconds.
- **Maintainability**: By defining our infrastructure as code using Terraform, we have made it simple to manage our cluster in the future. By setting up a build process for the AMI used by our node machines, we are able to quickly rebuild the image to pull in security updates and updated versions of our node software.

Sorry My App Ate the Cluster

8

Using Kubernetes to run our applications allows us to achieve much higher utilization of resources on the machines in our clusters. The Kubernetes scheduler is very effective at packing different applications onto your cluster in a way that will maximize the use of the resources on each machine. You can schedule a mix of lower-priority jobs that can be restarted if needed, for example, batch jobs, and high-priority jobs, such as web servers or databases. Kubernetes will help you make use of the idle CPU cycles that occur when your web server is waiting for requests.

This is great news if you want to reduce the amount that you are paying AWS, for your EC2 instances to run your applications. It is important to learn how to configure your pods, so Kubernetes can account for the resource use of your applications. If you don't configure your pods correctly, then the reliability and performance of your application could be impacted as Kubernetes may need to evict your pods from a node because it is running out of resources.

In this chapter, you are going to start by learning how to account for the memory and CPU that your pods will use. We will learn how to configure pods with a different quality of service so important workloads are guaranteed the resources they need, but less important workloads can make use of idle resources when they are available without needing dedicated resources. You will also learn how to make use of Kubernetes autoscaling facilities to add additional pods to your applications when they are under increased load, and to add additional nodes to your cluster when resources run low.

In this chapter, you will learn how to do the following:

- Configure container resource requests and limits
- Configure your pods for a desired **Quality of Service** (**QoS**) class
- Set quotas on the use of resources per namespace
- Use the horizontal pod autoscaler to automatically scale your applications to match the demand for them
- Use the cluster autoscaler to automatically provision and terminate EC2 instances as the use of your cluster changes over time

Resource requests and limits

Kubernetes allows us to achieve high utilization of our cluster by scheduling multiple different workloads to a single pool of machines. Whenever we ask Kubernetes to schedule a pod, it needs to consider which node to place it on. The scheduler can make much better decisions about where to place a pod if we can give it some information about the resources that the pod will need; it then can calculate the current workload on each node and choose the node that fits the expected resource usage of our pod. We can optionally give Kubernetes this information with resource **requests**. Requests are considered at the time when a pod is scheduled to a node. Requests do not provide any limit to the amount of resources a pod may consume once it is running on a particular node, they just represent an accounting of the requests that we, the cluster operator, made when we asked for a particular pod to be scheduled to the cluster.

In order to prevent pods from using more resources than they should, we can set resource **limits**. These limits can be enforced by the container runtime, to ensure that a pod doesn't use more of a particular resource than required.

We can say that the CPU use of a container is compressible because if we limit it, it might result in our processes running more slowly, but typically won't cause any other ill effects, whereas the memory use of a container is uncompressible, because the only remedy available if a container uses more than its memory limit is to kill the container in question.

It is very simple to add the configuration for resource limits and requests to a pod specification. In our manifests, each container specification can have a `resources` field that contains requests and limits. In this example, we request that an Nginx web server container is allocated 250 MiB of RAM and a quarter of a CPU core. Because the limit is set higher than the request, this allows the pod to use up to half a CPU core, and the container will only be killed if its memory use exceeds 128 Mi:

```
apiVersion: v1
kind: Pod
metadata:
  name: webserver
spec:
  containers:
  - name: nginx
    image: nginx
    resources:
      limits:
        memory: 128Mi
        cpu: 500m
      requests:
```

```
memory: 64Mi
cpu: 250m
```

Resource units

Whenever we specify CPU requests or limits, we specify them in terms of CPU cores. Because often we want to request or limit the use of a pod to some fraction of a whole CPU core, we can either specify this fraction of a CPU as a decimal or as a millicore value. For example, a value of 0.5 represents half of a core. It is also possible to configure requests or limits with a millicore value. As there are 1,000 millicores to a single core, we could specify half a CPU as 500 m. The smallest amount of CPU that can be specified is 1 m or 0.001.

I find that it can be more readable to use the millicore units in your manifests. When using `kubectl` or the Kubernetes dashboard, you will also notice that CPU limits and requests are formatted as millicore values. But if you are creating manifests with an automated process, you might use the floating point version.

Limits and requests for memory are measured in bytes. But specifying them in this way in your manifests would be quite unwieldy and difficult to read. So, Kubernetes supports the standard prefixes for referring to multiples of bytes; you can choose to use either a decimal multiplier such as M or G, or one of the binary equivalents, such as Mi or Gi, which are more commonly used as they reflect the actual size of the physical RAM.

The binary versions of these units are actually what most people really mean when they are talking about megabytes or gigabytes, even though more correctly they are talking about mebibytes and gibibytes!

In practice, you should just always remember to use the units with an **i** on the end, or you will end up with slightly less memory than you expected. This notation was introduced in the ISO/IEC 80000 standard in 1998, in order to avoid confusion between the decimal and binary units.

Decimal			Binary		
Name	Bytes	Suffix	Name	Bytes	Suffix
kilobyte	1000	K	kibibyte	1024	Ki
megabyte	1000^2	M	mebibyte	1024^2	Mi
gigabyte	1000^3	G	gibibyte	1024^3	Gi
terabyte	1000^4	T	tebibyte	1024^4	Ti

| petabyte | 1000^5 | P | pebibyte | 1024^5 | Pi |
| exabyte | 1000^6 | E | exbibyte | 1024^6 | Ei |

The memory units supported by Kubernetes

How pods with resource limits are managed

When the Kubelet starts a container, the CPU and memory limits are passed to the container runtime, which is then responsible for managing the resource usage of that container.

If you are using Docker, the CPU limit (in milicores) is multiplied by 100 to give the amount of CPU time the container will be allowed to use every 100 ms. If the CPU is under load, once a container has used its quota it will have to wait until the next 100 ms period before it can continue to use the CPU.

The method used to share CPU resources between different processes running in cgroups is called the **Completely Fair Scheduler** or **CFS**; this works by dividing CPU time between the different cgroups. This typically means assigning a certain number of slices to a cgroup. If the processes in one cgroup are idle and don't use their allocated CPU time, these shares will become available to be used by processes in other cgroups.

This means that a pod might perform well even if the limit is set too low, but could then grind to a halt only later, when another pod begins to take its fair share of allocated CPU. You may find that if you begin to set CPU limits on your pods on an empty cluster and add additional workloads, the performance of your pods begins to suffer.

Later in this chapter, we discuss some basic tooling that can give us an idea of how much CPU each pod is using.

If memory limits are reached, the container runtime will kill the container (and it might be restarted). If a container is using more memory than the requested amount, it becomes a candidate for eviction if and when the node begins to run low on memory.

Quality of Service (QoS)

When Kubernetes creates a pod, it is assigned one of three QoS classes. These classes are used to decide how Kubernetes schedules and evicts pods from nodes. Broadly, pods with a guaranteed QoS class will be subject to the least amount of disruption from evictions, and pods with the BestEffort QoS class are the most likely to be disrupted:

- **Guaranteed**: This is for high-priority workloads that benefit from avoiding being evicted from a node wherever possible and have priority over pods in the lower QoS classes for CPU resources, with the container runtime guaranteeing that the full amount of the CPU specified in the limit will be available when needed.

- **Burstable**: This is for less important workloads, for example, background jobs that can take advantage of greater CPU when available but are only guaranteed the level specified in the CPU request. Burstable pods are more likely to be evicted from a node than those in the Guaranteed QoS class when the node is running low on resources, especially if they are using more than the requested amount of memory.

- **BestEffort**: Pods with this class are the most likely to be evicted if a node is running low on resources. Pods in this QoS class can also only use whatever CPU and memory are free on the node at that time, so if other pods running on the node are making heavy use of the CPU, these pods may end up completely starved of resources. If you schedule Pods in this class, you should ensure that your application behaves as expected when subject to resource starvation and frequent restarts.

    In practice, it is always best to avoid using pods with a BestEffort QoS class, as these pods will be subject to very unusual behavior when the cluster is under heavy load.

When we set the resource and request limits on the containers in our pod, the combination of the values decides the QoS class the pod will be in.

To be given a QoS class of BestEffort, none of the containers in the pod should have any CPU or memory requests or limits set:

```
apiVersion: v1
kind: Pod
metadata:
  name: best-effort
spec:
  containers:
  - name: nginx
    image: nginx
```

A pod with no resource limits or requests will be assigned the BestEffort QoS class.

To be given a QoS class of Guaranteed, a pod needs to have both CPU and memory requests and limits set on each container in the pod. The limits and requests must match each other. As a shortcut, if a container only has its limits set, Kubernetes automatically assigns equal values to the resource requests:

```
apiVersion: v1
kind: Pod
metadata:
  name: guaranteed
spec:
  containers:
  - name: nginx
    image: nginx
    resources:
      limits:
        memory: 256Mi
        cpu: 500m
```

A pod that will be assigned the Guaranteed QoS class.

Anything that falls between these two cases will be given a QoS class of Burstable. This applies to any pod where any CPU or memory limits or requests have been set on any pods. But where they do not meet the criteria for the Guaranteed class, for example by not setting both limits on each container, or by having requests and limits that do not match:

```
apiVersion: v1
kind: Pod
metadata:
  name: burstable
spec:
  containers:
  - name: nginx
    image: nginx
    resources:
      limits:
        memory: 256Mi
        cpu: 500m
      requests:
        memory: 128Mi
        cpu: 250m
```

A pod that will be assigned the Burstable QoS class.

Resource quotas

Resource quotas allow you to place limits on how many resources a particular namespace can use. Depending on how you have chosen to use namespaces in your organization, they can give you a powerful way to limit the resources that are used by a particular team, application, or group of applications, while still giving developers the freedom to tweak the resource limits of each individual container.

Resource quotas are a useful tool when you want to control the resource costs of different teams or applications, but still want to achieve the utilization benefits of scheduling multiple workloads to the same cluster.

In Kubernetes, resource quotas are managed by an admission controller. This controller tracks the use of resources such as pods and services, and if a limit is exceeded, it prevents new resources from being created.

The resource quota admission controller is configured by one or more `ResourceQuota` objects created in the namespace. These objects would typically be created by a cluster administrator, but you could integrate creating them into a wider process in your organization for allocating resources.

Let's look at an example of how a quota can be used to limit the use of CPU resources in a cluster. As quotas will affect all the pods within a namespace, we will start by creating a new namespace using `kubectl`:

```
$ kubectl create namespace quota-example
namespace/quota-example created
```

We will start by creating a simple example that will ensure that every new pod that is created has the CPU limit set, and that the total limits do not exceed two cores:

```
apiVersion: v1
kind: ResourceQuota
metadata:
  name: resource-quota
  namespace: quota-example
spec:
  hard:
    limits.cpu: 2
```

Create the `ResourceQuota` by submitting the manifest to the cluster using `kubectl`.

 Once a `ResourceQuota` specifying resource requests or limits has been created in a namespace, it becomes mandatory for all pods to specify a corresponding request or limit before they can be created.

To see this behavior in action, let's create an example deployment in our namespace:

```
apiVersion: apps/v1
kind: Deployment
metadata:
  name: example
  namespace: quota-example
spec:
  selector:
    matchLabels:
      app: example
  template:
    metadata:
      labels:
        app: example
    spec:
      containers:
      - name: nginx
        image: nginx
        resources:
          limits:
            cpu: 500m
```

Once you have submitted the deployment manifest to Kubernetes with `kubectl`, check that the pod is running:

```
$ kubectl -n quota-example get pods
NAME                      READY     STATUS     RESTARTS    AGE
example-fb556779d-4bzgd   1/1       Running    0           1m
```

Now, scale up the deployment and observe that additional pods are created:

```
$ kubectl -n quota-example scale deployment/example --replicas=4$ kubectl -
n quota-example get pods
NAME                      READY     STATUS     RESTARTS    AGE
example-fb556779d-4bzgd   1/1       Running    0           2m
example-fb556779d-bpxm8   1/1       Running    0           1m
example-fb556779d-gkbvc   1/1       Running    0           1m
example-fb556779d-lcrg9   1/1       Running    0           1m
```

Because we specified a CPU limit of 500m, there is no problem scaling our deployment to four replicas, which uses the two cores that we specified in our quota.

But if you now try to scale the deployment so it uses more resources than specified in the quota, you will find that additional pods are not scheduled by Kubernetes:

```
$ kubectl -n quota-example scale deployment/example --replicas=5
```

Running `kubectl get events` will show you a message where the scheduler failed to create the additional pod required to meet the replica count:

```
$ kubectl -n quota-example get events
...
Error creating: pods "example-fb556779d-xmsgv" is forbidden: exceeded
quota: resource-quota, requested: limits.cpu=500m, used: limits.cpu=2,
limited: limits.cpu=2
```

Default limits

When you are using quotas on a namespace, one requirement is that every container in the namespace must have resource limits and requests defined. Sometimes this requirement can cause complexity and make it more difficult to work quickly with Kubernetes. Specifying resource limits correctly, while an essential part of preparing an application for production, does add additional overhead when, for example, using Kubernetes as a platform for development or testing workloads.

Kubernetes provides the facility for default requests and limits to be provided at the namespace level. You could use this to provide some sensible defaults to namespaces used by a particular application or team.

We can configure default limits and requests for the containers in a namespace using the `LimitRange` object. This object allows us to provide defaults for the CPU or memory, or both. If a `LimitRange` object exists in a namespace, then any container created without the resource requests or limits configured in `LimitRange` will inherit these values from the limit range.

There are two situations where `LimitRange` will affect the resource limits or requests when a pod is created:

- Containers that have no resource limits or requests will inherit the resource limit and requests from the `LimitRange` object
- Containers that have no resource limits but do have requests specified will inherit the resource limit from the `LimitRange` object

If a container already has limits and requests defined, then `LimitRange` will have no effect. Because containers that specify only limits default the request field to the same value, they will not inherit the request value from `LimitRange`. Let's look at a quick example of this in action. We start by creating a new namespace:

```
$ kubectl create namespace limit-example
namespace/limit-example created
```

Create a manifest for the limit range object, and submit it to the cluster with `kubectl`:

```
apiVersion: v1
kind: LimitRange
metadata:
  name: example
  namespace: limit-example
spec:
  limits:
  - default:
      memory: 512Mi
      cpu: 1
    defaultRequest:
      memory: 256Mi
      cpu: 500m
    type: Container
```

If you create a pod in this namespace without resource limits, it will inherit from the limit range object when they are created:

```
$ kubectl -n limit-example run --image=nginx example
```

`deployment.apps/` example created.

You can check the limits by running `kubectl describe`:

```
$ kubectl -n limit-example describe pods
...
    Limits:
      cpu:      1
      memory:   512Mi
    Requests:
      cpu:          500m
      memory:       256Mi
...
```

Horizontal Pod Autoscaling

Some applications can be scaled up to handle an increased load by adding additional replicas. Stateless web applications are a great example of this, as adding additional replicas provides the additional capacity required to handle increased requests to your application. Some other applications are also designed to operate in such a way that adding additional pods can handle increased loads; many systems that are architected around processing messages from a central queue can also handle an increased load in this way.

When we use Kubernetes deployments to deploy our pod workloads, it is simple to scale the number of replicas used by our applications up and down using the `kubectl scale` command. However, if we want our applications to automatically respond to changes in their workloads and scale to meet demand, then Kubernetes provides us with Horizontal Pod Autoscaling.

Horizontal Pod Autoscaling allows us to define rules that will scale the numbers of replicas up or down in our deployments based on CPU utilization and optionally other custom metrics. Before we are able to use Horizontal Pod Autoscaling in our cluster, we need to deploy the Kubernetes metrics server; this server provides endpoints that are used to discover CPU utilization and other metrics generated by our applications.

Deploying the metrics server

Before we can make use of Horizontal Pod Autoscaling, we need to deploy the Kubernetes metrics server to our cluster. This is because the Horizontal Pod Autoscaling controller makes use of the metrics provided by the `metrics.k8s.io` API, which is provided by the metrics server.

While some installations of Kubernetes may install this add-on by default, in our EKS cluster we will need to deploy it ourselves.

There are a number of ways to deploy add-on components to your cluster:

- If you have followed the advice in `Chapter 7`, *A Production-Ready Cluster*, and are provisioning your cluster with Terraform, you could provision the required manifests with `kubectl` as we did in `Chapter 7`, *A Production-Ready Cluster*, when we provisioned kube2iam.
- If you are using helm to manage applications on your cluster, you could use the stable/metrics server chart.

- In this chapter, for simplicity we are just going to deploy the metrics server manifests using `kubectl`.
- I like to integrate deploying add-ons such as the metrics server and kube2iam with the process that provisions the cluster, as I see them as integral parts of the cluster infrastructure. But if you are going to use a tool like helm to manage deploying applications to your cluster, then you might prefer to manage everything running on your cluster with the same tool. The decision you take really depends on the processes you and your team adopt for managing your cluster and the applications that run on it.
- The metrics server is developed in the GitHub repository found at `https://github.com/kubernetes-incubator/metrics-server` You will find the manifests required to deploy it in the deploy directory of that repository.

Start by cloning the configuration from GitHub. The metrics server began supporting the authentication methods provided by EKS in version 0.0.3 so make sure the manifests you have use at least that version.

You will find a number of manifests in the `deploy/1.8+` directory. The `auth-reader.yaml` and `auth-delegator.yaml` files configure the integration of the metrics server with the Kubernetes authorization infrastructure. The `resource-reader.yaml` file configures a role to give the metrics server the permissions to read resources from the API server, in order to discover the nodes that pods are running on. Basically, `metrics-server-deployment.yaml` and `metrics-server-service.yaml` define the deployment used to run the service itself and a service to be able to access it. Finally, the `metrics-apiservice.yaml` file defines an `APIService` resource that registers the metrics.k8s.io API group with the Kubernetes API server aggregation layer; this means that requests to the API server for the metrics.k8s.io group will be proxied to the metrics server service.

Deploying these manifests with `kubectl` is simple, just submit all of the manifests to the cluster with `kubectl apply`:

```
$ kubectl apply -f deploy/1.8+
```

You should see a message about each of the resources being created on the cluster.

If you are using a tool like Terraform to provision your cluster, you might use it to submit the manifests for the metrics server when you create your cluster.

Verifying the metrics server and troubleshooting

Before we continue, we should take a moment to check that our cluster and the metrics server are correctly configured to work together.

After the metrics server is running on your cluster and has had a chance to collect metrics from the cluster (give it a minute or so), you should be able to use the `kubectl top` command to see the resource usage of the pods and nodes in your cluster.

Start by running `kubectl top nodes`. If you see output like this, then the metrics server is configured correctly and is collecting metrics from your nodes:

```
$ kubectl top nodes
NAME            CPU(cores)    CPU%    MEMORY(bytes)    MEMORY%
ip-10-3-29-209  20m           1%      717Mi            19%
ip-10-3-61-119  24m           1%      1011Mi           28%
```

If you see an error message, then there are a number of troubleshooting steps you can follow.

You should start by describing the metrics server deployment and checking that one replica is available:

```
kubectl -n kube-system describe deployment metrics-server
```

If it is not, you should debug the created pod by running `kubectl -n kube-system describe pod`. Look at the events to see why the server is not available. Make sure that you are running at least version 0.0.3 of the metrics server, as previous versions didn't support authenticating with the EKS API server.

If the metrics server is running correctly and you still see errors when running `kubectl top`, the issue is that the APIservice registered with the aggregation layer is not configured correctly. Check the events output at the bottom of the information returned when you run `kubectl describe apiservice v1beta1.metrics.k8s.io`.

One common issue is that the EKS control plane cannot connect to the metrics server service on port `443`. If you followed the instructions in `Chapter 7`, *A Production-Ready Cluster*, you should already have a security group rule allowing this traffic from the control plane to the worker nodes, but some other documentation can suggest more restrictive rules, which might not allow traffic on port `443`.

Autoscaling pods based on CPU usage

Once the metrics server has been installed into our cluster, we will be able to use the metrics API to retrieve information about CPU and memory usage of the pods and nodes in our cluster. Using the `kubectl top` command is a simple example of this.

The Horizontal Pod Autoscaler can also use this same metrics API to gather information about the current resource usage of the pods that make up a deployment.

Let's look at an example of this; we are going to deploy a sample application that uses a lot of CPU under load, then configure a Horizontal Pod Autoscaler to scale up extra replicas of this pod to provide extra capacity when CPU utilization exceeds a target level.

The application we will be deploying as an example is a simple Ruby web application that can calculate the nth number in the Fibonacci sequence, this application uses a simple recursive algorithm, and is not very efficient (perfect for us to experiment with autoscaling). The deployment for this application is very simple. It is important to set resource limits for CPU because the target CPU utilization is based on a percentage of this limit:

```
deployment.yaml
apiVersion: apps/v1
kind: Deployment
metadata:
  name: fib
  labels:
    app: fib
spec:
  selector:
    matchLabels:
      app: fib
  template:
    metadata:
      labels:
        app: fib
    spec:
      containers:
      - name: fib
        image: errm/fib
        ports:
        - containerPort: 9292
        resources:
          limits:
            cpu: 250m
            memory: 32Mi
```

We are not specifying a number of replicas in the deployment spec; when we first submit this deployment to the cluster, the number of replicas will therefore default to 1. This is good practice when creating a deployment where we intend the replicas to be adjusted by a Horizontal Pod Autoscaler, because it means that if we use `kubectl apply` to update the deployment later, we won't override the replica value the Horizontal Pod Autoscaler has set (inadvertently scaling the deployment down or up).

Let's deploy this application to the cluster:

```
kubectl apply -f deployment.yaml
```

You could run `kubectl get pods -l app=fib` to check that the application started up correctly.

We will create a service, so we are able to access the pods in our deployment, requests will be proxied to each of the replicas, spreading the load:

```
service.yaml
kind: Service
apiVersion: v1
metadata:
  name: fib
spec:
  selector:
    app: fib
  ports:
  - protocol: TCP
    port: 80
    targetPort: 9292
```

Submit the service manifest to the cluster with `kubectl`:

```
kubectl apply -f service.yaml
```

We are going to configure a Horizontal Pod Autoscaler to control the number of replicas in our deployment. The `spec` defines how we want the autoscaler to behave; we have defined here that we want the autoscaler to maintain between 1 and 10 replicas of our application and achieve a target average CPU utilization of 60, across those replicas.

When CPU utilization falls below 60%, then the autoscaler will adjust the replica count of the targeted deployment down; when it goes above 60%, replicas will be added:

```
hpa.yaml
kind: HorizontalPodAutoscaler
apiVersion: autoscaling/v2beta1
metadata:
  name: fib
spec:
  maxReplicas: 10
  minReplicas: 1
  scaleTargetRef:
    apiVersion: app/v1
    kind: Deployment
    name: fib
  metrics:
  - type: Resource
    resource:
      name: cpu
      targetAverageUtilization: 60
```

Create the autoscaler with `kubectl`:

```
kubectl apply -f hpa.yaml
```

The `kubectl autoscale` command is a shortcut to create a `HorizontalPodAutoscaler`. **Running** `kubectl autoscale deployment fib --min=1 --max=10 --cpu-percent=60` would create an equivalent autoscaler.

Once you have created the Horizontal Pod Autoscaler, you can see a lot of interesting information about its current state with `kubectl describe`:

```
$ kubectl describe hpa fib
Name:              fib
Namespace:         default
CreationTimestamp: Sat, 15 Sep 2018 14:32:46 +0100
Reference:         Deployment/fib
Metrics:           ( current / target )
  resource cpu:    0% (1m) / 60%
Min replicas:      1
Max replicas:      10
Deployment pods:   1 current / 1 desired
```

Now we have set up our Horizontal Pod Autoscaler, we should generate some load on the pods in our deployment to illustrate how it works. In this case, we are going to use the `ab` (Apache benchmark) tool to repeatedly ask our application to compute the thirtieth Fibonacci number:

```
load.yaml
apiVersion: batch/v1
kind: Job
metadata:
  name: fib-load
  labels:
    app: fib
    component: load
spec:
  template:
    spec:
      containers:
      - name: fib-load
        image: errm/ab
        args: ["-n1000", "-c4", "fib/30"]
      restartPolicy: OnFailure
```

This job uses `ab` to make 1,000 requests to the endpoint (with a concurrency of 4). Submit the job to the cluster, then observe the state of the Horizontal Pod Autoscaler:

```
kubectl apply -f load.yaml
watch kubectl describe hpa fib
```

Once the load job has started to make requests, the autoscaler will scale up the deployment in order to handle the load:

```
Name:                 fib
Namespace:            default
CreationTimestamp:    Sat, 15 Sep 2018 14:32:46 +0100
Reference:            Deployment/fib
Metrics:              ( current / target )
  resource cpu:       100% (251m) / 60%
Min replicas:         1
Max replicas:         10
Deployment pods:      2 current / 2 desired
```

Autoscaling pods based on other metrics

The metrics server provides APIs that the Horizontal Pod Autoscaler can use to gain information about the CPU and memory utilization of pods in the cluster.

It is possible to target a utilization percentage like we did for the CPU metric, or to target the absolute value as we have here for the memory metric:

```
hpa.yaml
kind: HorizontalPodAutoscaler
apiVersion: autoscaling/v2beta1
metadata:
  name: fib
spec:
  maxReplicas: 10
  minReplicas: 1
  scaleTargetRef:
    apiVersion: app/v1
    kind: Deployment
    name: fib
  metrics:
  - type: Resource
    resource:
      name: memory
      targetAverageValue: 20M
```

The Horizonal Pod Autoscaler also allows us to scale on other metrics provided by more comprehensive metrics systems. Kubernetes allows for metrics APIs to be aggregated for custom and external metrics.

Custom metrics are metrics other than CPU and memory that are associated with a pod. You might for example use an adapter that allows you to use metrics that a system like Prometheus has collected from your pods.

This can be very beneficial if you have more detailed metrics available about the utilization of your application, for example, a forking web server that exposes a count of busy worker processes, or a queue processing application that exposes metrics about the number of items currently enqueued.

External metrics adapters provide information about resources that are not associated with any object within Kubernetes, for example, if you were using an external queuing system, such as the AWS SQS service.

On the whole, it is simpler if your applications can expose metrics about resources that they depend on that use an external metrics adapter, as it can be hard to limit access to particular metrics, whereas custom metrics are tied to a particular Pod, so Kubernetes can limit access to only those users and processes that need to use them.

Autoscaling the cluster

The capabilities of Kubernetes Horizontal Pod Autoscaler allow us to add and remove pod replicas from our applications as their resource usage changes over time. However, this makes no difference to the capacity of our cluster. If our pod autoscaler is adding pods to handle an increase in load, then eventually we might run out of space in our cluster, and additional pods would fail to be scheduled. If there is a decrease in the load on our application and the pod autoscaler removes pods, then we are paying AWS for EC2 instances that will sit idle.

When we created our cluster in `Chapter 7`, *A Production-Ready Cluster*, we deployed the cluster nodes using an autoscaling group, so we should be able to use this to grow and shrink the cluster as the needs of the applications deployed to it change over time.

Autoscaling groups have built-in support for scaling the size of the cluster, based on the average CPU utilization of the instances. This, however, is not really suitable when dealing with a Kubernetes cluster because the workloads running on each node of our cluster might be quite different, so the average CPU utilization is not really a very good proxy for the free capacity of the cluster.

Thankfully, in order to schedule pods to nodes effectively, Kubernetes keeps track of the capacity of each node and the resources requested by each pod. By utilizing this information, we can automate scaling the cluster to match the size of the workload.

The Kubernetes autoscaler project provides a cluster autoscaler component for some of the main cloud providers, including AWS. The cluster autoscaler can be deployed to our cluster quite simply. As well as being able to add instances to our cluster, the cluster autoscaler is also able to drain the pods from and then terminate instances when the capacity of the cluster can be reduced.

Deploying the cluster autoscaler

Deploying the cluster autoscaler to our cluster is quite simple as it just requires a simple pod to be running. All we need for this is a simple Kubernetes deployment, just as we have used in previous chapters.

In order for the cluster autoscaler to update the desired capacity of our autoscaling group, we need to give it permissions via an IAM role. If you are using kube2iam, as we discussed in Chapter 7, *A Production-Ready Cluster*, we will be able to specify this role for the cluster autoscaler pod via an appropriate annotation:

```
cluster_autoscaler.tf
data "aws_iam_policy_document" "eks_node_assume_role_policy" {
  statement {
    actions = ["sts:AssumeRole"]
    principals {
      type = "AWS"
      identifiers = ["${aws_iam_role.node.arn}"]
    }
  }
}


resource "aws_iam_role" "cluster-autoscaler" {
  name = "EKSClusterAutoscaler"
  assume_role_policy =
"${data.aws_iam_policy_document.eks_node_assume_role_policy.json}"
}


data "aws_iam_policy_document" "autoscaler" {
  statement {
    actions = [
      "autoscaling:DescribeAutoScalingGroups",
      "autoscaling:DescribeAutoScalingInstances",
      "autoscaling:DescribeTags",
      "autoscaling:SetDesiredCapacity",
      "autoscaling:TerminateInstanceInAutoScalingGroup"
    ]
    resources = ["*"]
  }
}

resource "aws_iam_role_policy" "cluster_autoscaler" {
  name = "cluster-autoscaler"
  role = "${aws_iam_role.cluster_autoscaler.id}"
  policy = "${data.aws_iam_policy_document.autoscaler.json}"
}
```

In order to deploy the cluster autoscaler to our cluster, we will submit a deployment manifest using `kubectl`, in a similar way to how we deployed kube2iam in `Chapter 7`, *A Production-Ready Cluster*. We will use Terraform's templating system to produce the manifest.

We create a service account that is used by the autoscaler to connect to the Kubernetes API:

```
cluster_autoscaler.tpl
---
apiVersion: v1
kind: ServiceAccount
metadata:
  labels:
    k8s-addon: cluster-autoscaler.addons.k8s.io
    k8s-app: cluster-autoscaler
  name: cluster-autoscaler
  namespace: kube-system
```

The cluster autoscaler needs to read information about the current resource usage of the cluster, and needs to be able to evict pods from nodes that need to be removed from the cluster and terminated. Basically, `cluster-autoscalerClusterRole` provides the required permissions for these actions. The following is the code continuation for `cluster_autoscaler.tpl`:

```
---
apiVersion: rbac.authorization.k8s.io/v1beta1
kind: ClusterRole
metadata:
  name: cluster-autoscaler
  labels:
    k8s-addon: cluster-autoscaler.addons.k8s.io
    k8s-app: cluster-autoscaler
rules:
- apiGroups: [""]
  resources: ["events","endpoints"]
  verbs: ["create", "patch"]
- apiGroups: [""]
  resources: ["pods/eviction"]
  verbs: ["create"]
- apiGroups: [""]
  resources: ["pods/status"]
  verbs: ["update"]
- apiGroups: [""]
  resources: ["endpoints"]
  resourceNames: ["cluster-autoscaler"]
  verbs: ["get","update"]
- apiGroups: [""]
```

```
    resources: ["nodes"]
    verbs: ["watch","list","get","update"]
  - apiGroups: [""]
    resources:
["pods","services","replicationcontrollers","persistentvolumeclaims","persi
stentvolumes"]
    verbs: ["watch","list","get"]
  - apiGroups: ["extensions"]
    resources: ["replicasets","daemonsets"]
    verbs: ["watch","list","get"]
  - apiGroups: ["policy"]
    resources: ["poddisruptionbudgets"]
    verbs: ["watch","list"]
  - apiGroups: ["apps"]
    resources: ["statefulsets"]
    verbs: ["watch","list","get"]
  - apiGroups: ["storage.k8s.io"]
    resources: ["storageclasses"]
    verbs: ["watch","list","get"]
---
apiVersion: rbac.authorization.k8s.io/v1beta1
kind: ClusterRoleBinding
metadata:
  name: cluster-autoscaler
  labels:
    k8s-addon: cluster-autoscaler.addons.k8s.io
    k8s-app: cluster-autoscaler
roleRef:
  apiGroup: rbac.authorization.k8s.io
  kind: ClusterRole
  name: cluster-autoscaler
subjects:
  - kind: ServiceAccount
    name: cluster-autoscaler
    namespace: kube-system
```

Note that `cluster-autoscaler` stores state information in a config map, so needs permissions to be able to read and write from it. This role allows that. The following is the code continuation for `cluster_autoscaler.tpl`:

```
---
apiVersion: rbac.authorization.k8s.io/v1beta1
kind: Role
metadata:
  name: cluster-autoscaler
  namespace: kube-system
  labels:
    k8s-addon: cluster-autoscaler.addons.k8s.io
```

```
      k8s-app: cluster-autoscaler
rules:
- apiGroups: [""]
  resources: ["configmaps"]
  verbs: ["create"]
- apiGroups: [""]
  resources: ["configmaps"]
  resourceNames: ["cluster-autoscaler-status"]
  verbs: ["delete","get","update"]
---
apiVersion: rbac.authorization.k8s.io/v1beta1
kind: RoleBinding
metadata:
  name: cluster-autoscaler
  namespace: kube-system
  labels:
    k8s-addon: cluster-autoscaler.addons.k8s.io
    k8s-app: cluster-autoscaler
roleRef:
  apiGroup: rbac.authorization.k8s.io
  kind: Role
  name: cluster-autoscaler
subjects:
  - kind: ServiceAccount
    name: cluster-autoscaler
    namespace: kube-system
```

Finally, let's consider the manifest for the cluster autoscaler deployment itself. The cluster autoscaler pod contains a single container running the cluster autoscaler control loop. You will notice that we are passing some configuration to the cluster autoscaler as command-line arguments. Most importantly, the `--node-group-auto-discovery` flag allows the autoscaler to operate on autoscaling groups with the `kubernetes.io/cluster/<cluster_name>` tag that we set on our autoscaling group when we created the cluster in Chapter 7, *A Production-Ready Cluster*. This is convenient because we don't have to explicitly configure the autoscaler with our cluster autoscaling group.

 If your Kubernetes cluster has nodes in more than one availability zone and you are running pods that rely on being scheduled to a particular zone (for example, pods that are making use of EBS volumes), it is recommended to create an autoscaling group for each availability zone that you plan to use. If you use one autoscaling group that spans several zones, then the cluster autoscaler will be unable to specify the availability zone of the instances that it launches.

Here is the code continuation for `cluster_autoscaler.tpl`:

```
---
apiVersion: extensions/v1beta1
kind: Deployment
metadata:
  name: cluster-autoscaler
  namespace: kube-system
  labels:
    app: cluster-autoscaler
spec:
  replicas: 1
  selector:
    matchLabels:
      app: cluster-autoscaler
  template:
    metadata:
      annotations:
        iam.amazonaws.com/role: ${iam_role}
      labels:
        app: cluster-autoscaler
    spec:
      serviceAccountName: cluster-autoscaler
      containers:
        - image: k8s.gcr.io/cluster-autoscaler:v1.3.3
          name: cluster-autoscaler
          resources:
            limits:
              cpu: 100m
              memory: 300Mi
            requests:
              cpu: 100m
              memory: 300Mi
          command:
            - ./cluster-autoscaler
            - --v=4
            - --stderrthreshold=info
            - --cloud-provider=aws
            - --skip-nodes-with-local-storage=false
            - --expander=least-waste
            - --node-group-auto-
discovery=asg:tag=kubernetes.io/cluster/${cluster_name}
          env:
            - name: AWS_REGION
              value: ${aws_region}
          volumeMounts:
            - name: ssl-certs
              mountPath: /etc/ssl/certs/ca-certificates.crt
```

```
              readOnly: true
          imagePullPolicy: "Always"
      volumes:
        - name: ssl-certs
          hostPath:
            path: "/etc/ssl/certs/ca-certificates.crt"
```

Finally, we render the templated manifest by passing in the variables for the AWS region, cluster name and IAM role, and submitting the file to Kubernetes using `kubectl`:

Here is the code continuation for `cluster_autoscaler.tpl`:

```
data "aws_region" "current" {}

data "template_file" " cluster_autoscaler " {
  template = "${file("${path.module}/cluster_autoscaler.tpl")}"

  vars {
    aws_region = "${data.aws_region.current.name}"
    cluster_name = "${aws_eks_cluster.control_plane.name}"
    iam_role = "${aws_iam_role.cluster_autoscaler.name}"
  }
}

resource "null_resource" "cluster_autoscaler" {
  triggers = {
    manifest_sha1 =
"${sha1("${data.template_file.cluster_autoscaler.rendered}")}"
  }

  provisioner "local-exec" {
    command = "kubectl
--kubeconfig=${local_file.kubeconfig.filename} apply -f -
<<EOF\n${data.template_file.cluster_autoscaler.rendered}\nEOF"
  }
}
```

Summary

Kubernetes is a powerful tool; it is very effective at achieving much higher usage of compute resources than would ever be possible by manually scheduling applications to machines. It is important that you learn how to allocate resources to your pods by setting the correct resource limits and requests; if you don't, your applications can become unreliable or starved of resources.

By understanding how Kubernetes assigns Quality of Service classes to your pods based on the resource requests and limits that you assign them, you can have precisely control how your pods are managed. By ensuring your critical applications, such as web servers and databases, run with the Guaranteed class, you can ensure that they will perform consistently and suffer minimal disruption when pods need to be rescheduled. You can improve the efficiency of your cluster by setting limits on lower-priority pods that will result in them being scheduled with the Burstable QoS class. Burstable pods can use extra resources when they are available but won't need extra capacity to be added to the cluster when load increases.

Resource quotas can be invaluable when managing a large cluster that is used to run several applications, and even by different teams in your organization, especially if you are trying to control the cost of non-production workloads, such as testing and staging environments.

AWS calls its machines elastic for a reason: they can be scaled up or down in a matter of minutes to meet the demands of your applications. If you run workloads on a cluster where the load is variable, then you should make use of these properties and the tools that Kubernetes provides to scale your deployments to match the load that your applications are receiving, and your cluster to the size of the pods that need to be scheduled.

9
Storing State

This chapter is all about utilizing the deep integration that Kubernetes has with the AWS native storage solution **Elastic Block Store** (**EBS**). Amazon EBS provides network attached storage as a service, and is the primary solution used to provide block storage to EC2 instances.

Nearly every EC2 instance launched is backed by an EBS root volume (created from an AMI machine image). Because EBS storage is network attached, if an underlying machine hosting an EC2 instance fails in some way, the data stored on the volume is safe as it is automatically replicated across multiple physical storage devices.

In addition to being used to store the root filesystem of EC2 instances, additional EBS volumes can be attached to EC2 instances and mounted on demand via the AWS API. Kubernetes integration with AWS EBS makes use of this to provide persistent volumes that can be used by your pods. If a pod is killed and is replaced by a pod on another EC2 instance, Kubernetes will handle detaching the EBS volume from the old EC2 instance and attaching it to the new instance, ready to be mounted into the new pod as required.

In this chapter, we will start by looking at how we can configure our pods to make use of additional volumes. We will then look at the abstractions Kubernetes provides for dealing with storage that provides persistence (such as EBS). We will look at how Kubernetes can automatically provision EBS volumes for us based on the specifications requested in our pod configurations.

Once you have mastered using Kubernetes to provision persistent storage for your pods, in the second half of this chapter we will look at stateful sets, the abstraction that Kubernetes provides to run a set of pods, each of which can have its own attached storage and an identity that remains even if rescheduled to another node. This is the final piece of the puzzle required if you want to run complex stateful applications on your Kubernetes cluster, such as databases.

In this chapter, we will cover the following topics:

- Volumes
- Storage classes
- Stateful sets

Volumes

Let's start by looking at how we can attach volumes to our pods. The simplest kind of volume available emptyDir is just a temporary directory that is linked to the life cycle of a pod. When the volume is created, it is empty as the name suggests, and remains on the node until the pod is removed from the node. The data you store inside the volume does persist between pod restarts on the same node, so can be useful for processes that need to cache expensive computations on the filesystem, or for processes that checkpoint their progress. In Chapter 1, *Google's Infrastructure for the Rest of Us*, we discussed some other possible uses for an emptyDir volume to share files between different containers within a pod.

In this example, we are going to make use of an emptyDir volume to deploy an application that expects to write to the /data directory in a container where the root filesystem has been made read-only.

This application has been designed to illustrate some of the properties of volumes in Kubernetes. When it starts up, it writes to a random filename in the /data directory. It then starts up a web server that shows the contents of that directory:

```
apiVersion: apps/v1
kind: Deployment
metadata:
  name: randserver
spec:
  selector:
    matchLabels:
      app: randserver
  template:
    metadata:
      labels:
        app: example
    spec:
      containers:
      - image: errm/randserver
        name: randserver
        volumeMounts:
```

```
    - mountPath: /data
      name: data
    securityContext:
      readOnlyRootFilesystem: true
volumes:
- name: data
  emptyDir: {}
```

Looking at this configuration, there are a few things you should note about how we use volumes in a pod. These rules apply not only to `emptyDir` volumes, but also to every other type of volume that you might encounter:

- Each volume is defined at the top level of the pod spec. Even if a volume is used by more than one container in a pod, we only need to define it once.
- When you want to access a volume from within a container, you must specify a volume mount, mounting that volume into the container's filesystem at a particular point. When we mount a volume, we refer to it by the name we used when we defined it in the `volumes` section.

Once you have deployed this example manifest, you should be able to use the `kubectl port-forward` command to access the web server running inside the pod:

```
$ kubectl port-forward deployment/randserver 3000:3000
Forwarding from 127.0.0.1:3000 -> 3000
Forwarding from [::1]:3000 -> 3000
```

You should now be able to visit `http://localhost:3000` in your browser to see a random file that was created when the container started up:

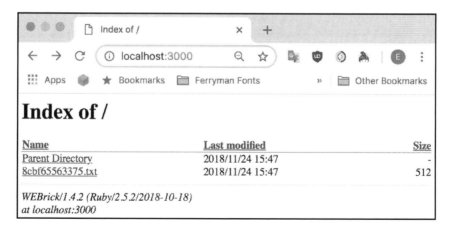

If you delete this pod, then the deployment will recreate a new pod. Because the contents of an `emptyDir` volume are lost whenever the pod is destroyed, the file that was created when the first pod started will be gone, and a new file with a different name will have been created:

```
$ kubectl delete pod -l app=randserver
pod "randserver-79559c5fb6-htnxm" deleted
```

You will need to rerun `kubectl port-forward` to select the new pod:

```
$ kubectl port-forward deployment/randserver 3000:3000
```

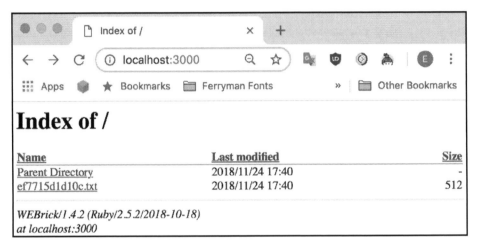

A newly created file being served

EBS volumes

Getting Kubernetes to attach an EBS volume and then mount it into a container in our pod is almost as simple as using an `emptyDir` volume. The lowest level and simplest way to mount an EBS volume is by using the `awsElasticBlockStore` volume type. This volume type handles attaching the EBS volume to the node where our pod will run and then mounting the volume into a path in our container.

When using this volume type, Kubernetes does not handle actually creating the volume for us, so we need to do this manually. We can do this using the AWS CLI:

```
$ aws ec2 create-volume --availability-zone=us-east-1a --size=5 --volume-type=gp2
{
    "AvailabilityZone": "us-east-1a",
    "CreateTime": "2018-11-17T15:17:54.000Z",
    "Encrypted": false,
    "Size": 5,
    "SnapshotId": "",
    "State": "creating",
    "VolumeId": "vol-04e744aad50d4911",
    "Iops": 100,
    "Tags": [],
    "VolumeType": "gp2"
}
```

Remember that EBS volumes are tied to a particular availability zone (just like `ec2` instances) and can only be attached to instances in that same availability zone, so you will need to create volume(s) in the same zone(s) as the instances in your cluster.

Here, we have updated the deployment we created in the last example to use the `awsElasticBlockStore` volume type and attach the volume we just created to our pod. The ID of the EBS volume is passed to the volume configuration as a parameter:

```
apiVersion: apps/v1
kind: Deployment
metadata:
  name: randserver
spec:
  selector:
    matchLabels:
      app: randserver
  template:
    metadata:
      labels:
        app: randserver
    spec:
      containers:
      - image: errm/randserver
        name: randserver
        volumeMounts:
        - mountPath: /data
          name: data
        securityContext:
          readOnlyRootFilesystem: true
```

```
volumes:
- name: data
  awsElasticBlockStore:
    volumeID: vol-04e744aad50d4911
    fsType: ext4
nodeSelector:
  "failure-domain.beta.kubernetes.io/zone": us-east-1a
```

You will see that manually attaching an EBS volume in this way is very similar to using the simpler `emptyDir` volume.

> The special `failure-domain.beta.kubernetes.io/zone` label is added to each node automatically by the AWS cloud provider. Here, we are using it in `nodeSelector` of our pod definition to schedule the pod to a node in the same availability zone as we created the volume in. There are several other labels that Kubernetes will automatically add to the nodes in your cluster. You can read about them in the Kubernetes documentation at
> `https://kubernetes.io/docs/reference/kubernetes-api/labels-annotations-taints/`.

When you first submit this deployment, its behavior will be exactly the same as the previous version. But when we delete the pod and it is replaced, you will notice that the file(s) created on the previous runs of this container will remain, and a new file will be added to the list every time it starts up:

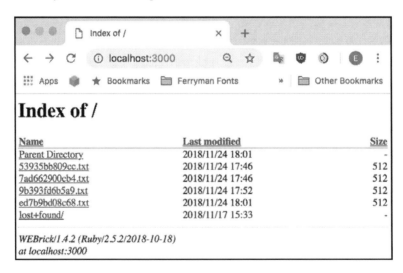

When our application is backed by an EBS volume, files survive pod rescheduling

Persistent volumes

While we certainly could manually create EBS volumes in this way and use their IDs in our manifests, there are some problems with this approach.

It is unwieldy and time consuming for users who want to run their applications on a cluster to first think about provisioning the EBS volumes that an application needs before modifying the manifests to refer to hardcoded IDs. It means that pod manifests will need to include a configuration that is specific to running the application in question on AWS. Ideally, we would want as much of our configuration as possible to be reusable between the different environments where we might deploy it, to avoid the risk of introducing errors caused by having to modify configurations.

Kubernetes provides two abstractions that will help us manage EBS volumes: PersistentVolume and PersistentVolumeClaim.

The PersistentVolume object represents a physical piece of storage in your cluster; on AWS this is an EBS volume, in much the same way that the Node object represents an EC2 instance in your cluster. The object captures the details of how the storage is implemented, so for an EBS volume it records its ID so that Kubernetes can attach it to the correct node when a pod using the volume is scheduled.

PersistentVolumeClaim is the Kubernetes object that allows us to express a request for PersistentVolume to be used in a pod. When we request a persistent volume, we only need to request the amount of storage we require and optionally a storage class (see the next section). PersistentVolumeClaim is normally embedded within a pod spec. When a pod is scheduled, its PersistentVolumeClaim is matched to a particular PersistentVolume that is big enough to fulfill the requested amount of storage. PersistentVolume is bound to its requesting PersistentVolumeClaim, so that even if a pod is rescheduled, the same underlying volume will be attached to the pod.

This is a big improvement over manually provisioning EBS volumes and including the volume ID in our configuration, because we don't need to modify our manifest every time our pod is deployed to a new environment.

If you were operating Kubernetes manually (for example, in a bare metal deployment) the cluster administrator might pre-provision a pool of PersistentVolume, which would then be matched against and bound to each PersistentVolumeClaim as they are created. When using AWS, there is no need to pre-provision storage, as Kubernetes dynamically creates PersistentVolume using the AWS API as they are required.

Persistent volumes example

Let's look at how we can use persistent volumes to simplify the deployment of our example application.

To avoid additional charges on your AWS account, you might want to delete the EBS volume you created manually in the previous example.

First, delete the deployment that we created so Kubernetes can detach the volume:

```
$ kubectl delete deployment/randserver
```

Then, you can use the AWS CLI to delete the EBS volume:

```
$ aws ec2 delete-volume --volume-id vol-04e744aad50d4911
```

Before you begin, make sure that you have added at least the general-purpose storage class to your cluster.

Creating an EBS volume using Kubernetes dynamic volume provisioning is as simple as creating any other resource with kubectl:

```
apiVersion: v1
kind: PersistentVolumeClaim
metadata:
  name: randserver-data
spec:
  accessModes:
    - ReadWriteOnce
  storageClassName: general-purpose
  resources:
    requests:
      storage: 1Gi
```

If you added the storageclass.kubernetes.io/is-default-class annotation to a storage class in your cluster, you could omit the storageClassName field if you wanted to.

Once you create `PersistantVolumeClaim` for a storage class using the `kubernetes.io/aws-ebs` provisioner, Kubernetes will provision an EBS volume matching the size and storage class parameters that you specified. Once this is completed, you can use `kubectl describe` to view the claim; you can see that the status has been updated to `Bound` and the `Volume` field shows the underlying `PersistentVolume` that the claim has been bound to:

```
$ kubectl describe pvc/randserver-data
Name:           randserver-data
Namespace:      default
StorageClass:   general-purpose
Status:         Bound
Volume:         pvc-5c2dab0d-f017-11e8-92ac-0a56f9f52542
Capacity:       1Gi
Access Modes:   RWO
```

If we use `kubectl describe` to inspect this `PersistentVolume`, we can see the details of the underlying EBS volume that was automatically provisioned:

```
$ kubectl describe pv/pvc-5c2dab0d-f017-11e8-92ac-0a56f9f52542
Name: pvc-5c2dab0d-f017-11e8-92ac-0a56f9f52542
StorageClass: general-purpose
Status: Bound
Claim: default/randserver-data
Reclaim Policy: Delete
Access Modes: RWO
Capacity: 1Gi
Source:
    Type: AWSElasticBlockStore (a Persistent Disk resource in AWS)
    VolumeID: aws://us-east-1a/vol-04ad625aa4d5da62b
    FSType: ext4
    Partition: 0
    ReadOnly: false
```

In our deployment, we can update the `volumes` section of the pod spec to refer to `PersistentVolumeClaim` by name:

```
apiVersion: apps/v1
kind: Deployment
metadata:
  name: randserver
spec:
  selector:
    matchLabels:
      app: randserver
  template:
    metadata:
```

```
    labels:
      app: randserver
  spec:
    containers:
    - image: errm/randserver
      name: randserver
      volumeMounts:
      - mountPath: /data
        name: data
      securityContext:
        readOnlyRootFilesystem: true
    volumes:
    - name: data
      persistentVolumeClaim:
        claimName: randserver-data
```

Storage classes

On AWS, there are several different types of volume available that offer different price and performance characteristics.

In order to provide a simple way to choose the volume type (and some other settings) when we provision a volume, we create a `StorageClass` object that we can then refer to by name when we create `PersistentVolumeClaim`.

Storage classes are created in the same way as any other Kubernetes objects, by submitting manifests to the API using `kubectl`:

```
kind: StorageClass
apiVersion: storage.k8s.io/v1
metadata:
  name: general-purpose
  annotations:
    "storageclass.kubernetes.io/is-default-class": "true"
provisioner: kubernetes.io/aws-ebs
parameters:
  type: gp2
```

This manifest creates a storage class called `general-purpose` that creates volumes with the `gp2` volume type. If you remember our discussion about EBS volume types in `Chapter 6`, *Planning for Production*, this SSD-backed volume type is suitable for most general-purpose applications offering a good balance of performance and price.

You will also notice the `storageclass.kubernetes.io/is-default-class` annotation that makes `StorageClass` the default one to be used by any `PersistentVolumeClaim` that doesn't specify a storage class. You should only apply this annotation to a single `StorageClass`.

The `parameter` field accepts several different options.

The most important parameter field is `type`, that allows us to choose one of `gp2` (the default), `io1` (provisioned IOPS), `sc1` (cold storage), or `st1` (throughput optimized).

If you choose to use the `io1` type, you should also use the `iopsPerGB` parameter to specify the number of IOPS that will be provisioned for each GB of disk storage requested. The maximum IOPS/GB ratio supported by `io1` EBS volumes is 50:1.

Bear in mind that the cost of provisioned IOPS makes the cost of `io1` volumes much higher than the equivalent general-purpose volumes. An `io1` volume with IOPS provisioned to provide similar throughput to a `gp2` volume of the same size can be three times more expensive. So, you should only use `io1` volumes where you require performance in excess of that provided by `gp2` volumes. One trick that can optimize costs is to use `gp2` volumes larger than your application requires to provide extra IO credits.

You could, for example, create several different classes using the `io1` type to be used by applications with different performance requirements:

```
kind: StorageClass
apiVersion: storage.k8s.io/v1
metadata:
  name: high-iops-ssd
provisioner: kubernetes.io/aws-ebs
parameters:
  type: io1
  iopsPerGB: "50"
---
 kind: StorageClass
apiVersion: storage.k8s.io/v1
metadata:
  name: medium-iops-ssd
provisioner: kubernetes.io/aws-ebs
parameters:
  type: io1
  iopsPerGB: "25"
```

Note that Kubernetes expects a string value for the `iopsPerGb` field, so you will need to quote this value.

If you are using an application that is optimized to make sequential reads and writes to the filesystem, then you might benefit from using the `st1` volume type, which uses optimized magnetic storage to provide high throughput reads and writes. It is not recommended to use this storage for general-purpose use, as the performance when making random access reads or writes will be poor:

```
kind: StorageClass
apiVersion: storage.k8s.io/v1
metadata:
  name: throughput
provisioner: kubernetes.io/aws-ebs
parameters:
  type: st1
```

The `sc1` volume type offers the very lowest cost storage available as an EBS volume and is intended for infrequently accessed data. Like `st1` volumes, `sc1` is optimized for sequential reads and writes, so will perform poorly on workloads with random reads and writes:

```
kind: StorageClass
apiVersion: storage.k8s.io/v1
metadata:
  name: cold-storage
provisioner: kubernetes.io/aws-ebs
parameters:
  type: sc1
```

It is a good idea to decide up front the different storage classes you want to make available in your cluster, and then provide documentation about when each class should be used to users of your cluster.

You should think about submitting a list of storage classes to your cluster as part of your provisioning process, as there are no storage classes created by default when you provision an EKS cluster.

StatefulSet

So far, we have seen how we can use Kubernetes to automatically provision EBS volumes for `PersistentVolumeClaim`. This can be very useful for a number of applications where we need a single volume to provide persistence to a single pod.

We run into problems though, as soon as we try to scale our deployment up. Pods running on the same node may end up sharing the volume. But as EBS volumes can only be attached to a single instance at any one time, any pods scheduled to another node will get stuck with the `ContainerCreating` status, waiting endlessly for the EBS volume to be attached.

If you are running an application where you want each replica to have its own unique volume, we can use a stateful set. Stateful sets have two key advantages over deployments when we want to deploy applications where each replica needs to have its own persistent storage.

Firstly, instead of referring to a single persistent volume by name, we can provide a template to create a new persistent volume for each pod. This allows us to provision an independent EBS volume for each pod replica, just by scaling up the stateful set. If we wanted to achieve this with a deployment, we would need to create a separate Deployment for each replica, each referring to a different persistent volume by name.

Secondly, when a pod is scheduled by `StatefulSet`, each replica has a consistent and persistent hostname that stays the same even if the pod is rescheduled to another node. This is very useful when running software where each replica expects to be able to connect to its peers at a specific address. Before stateful sets were added to Kubernetes, deploying such software to Kubernetes often relied on special plugins to perform service discovery using the Kubernetes API.

To illustrate how stateful sets work, we are going to rewrite our example application deployment manifest to use `StatefulSet`. Because each replica pod in `StatefulSet` has a predictable hostname, we first need to create a service to allow traffic to these hostnames to be routed to the underlying pods:

```
apiVersion: v1
kind: Service
metadata:
  name: randserver
  labels:
    app: randserver
spec:
  ports:
  - port: 80
    name: web
    targetPort: 3000
  clusterIP: None
  selector:
    app: randserver
```

Each pod will be given a hostname constructed from the name of the stateful set and the pod number in the set. The domain of the hostname is the name of the service.

Thus, when we create a stateful set called `randserver` with three replicas. The Pods in the set will be given the hostnames `randserver-0`, `randserver-1`, and `randserver-2`. Other services running inside the cluster will be able to connect to these pods by using the names `randserver-0.randserver`, `randserver-1.randserver`, and `randserver-2.randserver`.

The configuration for `StatefulSet` is very similar to the configuration for a deployment. The key differences that should be noted are these:

- The `serviceName` field where we need to refer to the service used to provide network access to the pods.
- The `volumeClaimTemplates` field where we include a template for `PersistentVolumeClaim` that will be created for each pod replica in `StatefulSet`. You can think of this as an analog to the template field that provides a template for each pod that is created:

```
apiVersion: apps/v1
kind: StatefulSet
metadata:
  name: randserver
spec:
  selector:
    matchLabels:
      app: randserver
  serviceName: randserver
  replicas: 3
  template:
    metadata:
      labels:
        app: randserver
    spec:
      containers:
      - image: errm/randserver
        name: randserver
        volumeMounts:
        - mountPath: /data
          name: data
        securityContext:
          readOnlyRootFilesystem: true
  volumeClaimTemplates:
    - metadata:
        name: data
```

```
spec:
  accessModes:
    - ReadWriteOnce
  storageClassName: general-purpose
  resources:
    requests:
      storage: 1Gi
```

Once you have submitted `StatefulSet` to Kubernetes, you should be able to see the pods that have successfully been scheduled to the cluster:

```
$ kubectl get pods
NAME           READY    STATUS     RESTARTS    AGE
randserver-0   1/1      Running    0           39s
randserver-1   1/1      Running    0           21s
randserver-2   1/1      Running    0           10s
```

Note that the name of each pod follows a predictable pattern, unlike pods created with a deployment or replica set, which each have a random name.

Try deleting one of the pods in the stateful set, and notice that it is replaced by a pod with exactly the same name as the one that was deleted:

```
$ kubectl delete pod/randserver-1
$ kubectl get pods
NAME           READY    STATUS     RESTARTS    AGE
randserver-0   1/1      Running    0           17m
randserver-1   1/1      Running    0           18s
randserver-2   1/1      Running    0           17m
```

If you look at the persistent volume claims, you will see that their names also follow a predictable pattern where the name of a claim is formed from the name given in the volume claim template metadata, the name of the stateful set, and the pod number:

```
kubectl get pvc
NAME                STATUS    VOLUME
data-randserver-0   Bound     pvc-803210cf-f027-11e8-b16d
data-randserver-1   Bound     pvc-99192c41-f027-11e8-b16d
data-randserver-2   Bound     pvc-ab2b25b1-f027-11e8-b16d
```

If you delete (or scale down) a stateful set, then the associated persistent volume claims remain. This is quite advantageous as it makes it harder to lose the valuable data created by an application. If you later recreate (or scale up) the stateful set, then by virtue of the predictable names used, the same volumes are reused.

If you do intend to fully remove a stateful set from your cluster, you may also need to additionally remove the corresponding persistent volume claims:

```
$ kubectl delete statefulset randserver
statefulset.apps "randserver" deleted
$ kubectl delete pvc -l app=randserver
persistentvolumeclaim "data-randserver-0" deleted
persistentvolumeclaim "data-randserver-1" deleted
persistentvolumeclaim "data-randserver-2" deleted
```

Summary

In this chapter, we have learned about the rich set of tools that Kubernetes provides to provision storage for your applications.

You should have learned the following:

- How to configure volumes for your pods
- How to mount volumes into containers
- How to automatically provision EBS volumes with persistent volume claims
- How to provision different EBS volume types by configuring storage classes
- How to dynamically provision a volume for each pod in a stateful set

You should now have enough knowledge to deploy many types of applications to your Kubernetes cluster.

Further reading

If you want to learn more about how to utilize storage in Kubernetes, here are some resources that you might find useful:

- **Kubernetes Helm Charts include many configuration examples for well-known datastores that make extensive use of persistent volumes**: `https://github.com/helm/charts`
- **The Kubernetes documentation has detailed and extensive information about using storage in Kubernetes**: `https://kubernetes.io/docs/concepts/storage/`
- **The Kubernetes EFS provisioner provides an add-on provisioner that can be deployed to provision volumes backed by AWS Elastic File System (EFS). This can be a useful tool if you want multiple pods to be able to read and write from the same volume**: `https://github.com/kubernetes-incubator/external-storage/tree/master/aws/efs`

10
Managing Container Images

A container orchestration platform needs a solid foundation to run our containers. One vital piece of infrastructure is the location where we store our container images, which will allow us to reliably fetch them when creating our pods.

From a developer's point of view, it should be very easy and fast to push new images whilst developing the software we wish to deploy to Kubernetes. We'll also want to have mechanisms that help us with versioning, cataloging, and describing how to use our images, in order to facilitate deployments and reduce the risk of delivering the wrong version or configuration of our software.

Container images can often contain intellectual property, proprietary source code, infrastructure configuration secrets, and even business secrets. Therefore, we need to have proper authentication and authorization mechanisms to protect them from unwanted access.

In this chapter, we're going to learn how to leverage the AWS **Elastic Container Registry (ECR)** service to store our container images in a manner that tackles all these needs.

In this chapter, we will cover the following topics:

- Pushing Docker images to ECR
- Tagging images
- Labeling images

Pushing Docker images to ECR

Currently, the most commonly adopted way to store and deliver Docker images is through Docker Registry, an open source application by Docker that hosts Docker repositories. This application can be deployed on-premises, as well as used as a service from multiple providers, such as **Docker Hub**, **Quay.io**, and **AWS ECR**.

The application is a simple, stateless service, where most of the maintenance work involves making sure that storage is available, safe, and secure. As any seasoned system administrator knows, that is far from an easy ordeal, especially, if there is a large data store. For that reason, and especially if you're just starting out, it is highly recommended to use a hosted solution and let someone else deal with keeping your images safe and readily available.

ECR is AWS's approach to a hosted Docker registry, where there's one registry per account, uses AWS IAM to authenticate and authorize users to push and pull images. By default, the limits for both repositories and images are set to 1,000. As we'll see, the setup flow feels very similar to other AWS services, whilst also being familiar for Docker Registry users.

Creating a repository

To create a repository, it's as simple as executing the following `aws ecr` command:

```
$ aws ecr create-repository --repository-name randserver
```

This will create a repository for storing our `randserver` application. Its output should look like this:

```
{
  "repository": {
        "repositoryArn": "arn:aws:ecr:eu-
central-1:123456789012:repository/randserver",
        "registryId": "123456789012",
        "repositoryName": "randserver",
        "repositoryUri": "123456789012.dkr.ecr.eu-
central-1.amazonaws.com/randserver",
      "createdAt": 1543162198.0
  }
}
```

A nice addition to your repositories is a life cycle policy that cleans up older versions of your images, so that you don't eventually get blocked from pushing a newer version. This can be achieved as follows, using the same `aws ecr` command:

```
$ aws ecr put-lifecycle-policy --registry-id 123456789012 --repository-name
randserver --lifecycle-policy-text
'{"rules":[{"rulePriority":10,"description":"Expire old
images","selection":{"tagStatus":"any","countType":"imageCountMoreThan","co
untNumber":800},"action":{"type":"expire"}}]}'
```

This particular policy will start cleaning up once have more than 800 images on the same repository. You could also clean up based on the images, age, or both, as well as consider only some tags in your cleanup.

> For more information and examples, refer to `https://docs.aws.amazon.com/AmazonECR/latest/userguide/lifecycle_policy_examples.html`.

Pushing and pulling images from your workstation

In order use your newly-created ECR repository, first we're going to need to authenticate your local Docker daemon against the ECR registry. Once again, `aws ecr` will help you achieve just that:

```
aws ecr get-login --registry-ids 123456789012 --no-include-email
```

This will output a `docker login` command that will add a new user-password pair for your Docker configuration. You can copy-paste that command, or you can just run it as follows; the results will be the same:

```
$(aws ecr get-login --registry-ids 123456789012 --no-include-email)
```

Now, pushing and pulling images is just like using any other Docker registry, using the outputted repository URI that we got when creating the repository:

```
$ docker push 123456789012.dkr.ecr.eu-
central-1.amazonaws.com/randserver:0.0.1
$ docker pull 123456789012.dkr.ecr.eu-
central-1.amazonaws.com/randserver:0.0.1
```

Setting up privileges for pushing images

IAM users' permissions should allow your users to perform strictly only the operations they actually need to, in order to avoid any possible mistakes that might have a larger area of impact. This is also true for ECR management, and to that effect, there are three AWS IAM managed policies that greatly simplify achieving it:

- `AmazonEC2ContainerRegistryFullAccess`: This allows a user to perform any operation on your ECR repositories, including deleting them, and should therefore be left for system administrators and owners.
- `AmazonEC2ContainerRegistryPowerUser`: This allows a user to push and pull images on any repositories, which is very handy for developers that are actively building and deploying your software.
- `AmazonEC2ContainerRegistryReadOnly`: This allows a user to pull images on any repository, which is useful for scenarios where developers are not pushing their software from their workstation, and are instead just pulling internal dependencies to work on their projects.

All of these policies can be attached to an IAM user as follows, by replacing the policy name at the end of the ARN with a suitable policy (as described previously) and pointing --user-name to the user you are managing:

```
$ aws iam attach-user-policy --policy-arn
arn:aws:iam::aws:policy/AmazonEC2ContainerRegistryReadOnly  --user-name
johndoe
```

All these AWS managed policies do have an important characteristic—all of them add permissions for all repositories on your registry. You'll probably find several use cases where this is far from ideal—maybe your organization has several teams that do not need access over each other's repositories; maybe you would like to have a user with the power to delete some repositories, but not all; or maybe you just need access to a single repository for **Continuous Integration** (**CI**) setup.

If your needs match any of these described situations, you should create your own policies with as granular permissions as required.

First, we will create an IAM group for the developers of our `randserver` application:

```
$ aws iam create-group --group-name randserver-developers
    {
        "Group": {
        "Path": "/",
        "GroupName": "randserver-developers",
        "GroupId": "AGPAJRDMVLGOJF3ARET5K",
```

```
        "Arn": "arn:aws:iam::123456789012:group/randserver-developers",
        "CreateDate": "2018-10-25T11:45:42Z"
        }
    }
```

Then we'll add the johndoe user to the group:

```
$ aws iam add-user-to-group --group-name randserver-developers --user-name
johndoe
```

Now we'll need to create our policy so that we can attach it to the group. Copy this JSON document to a file:

```
{
    "Version": "2012-10-17",
    "Statement": [{
        "Effect": "Allow",
        "Action": [
            "ecr:GetAuthorizationToken",
            "ecr:BatchCheckLayerAvailability",
            "ecr:GetDownloadUrlForLayer",
            "ecr:GetRepositoryPolicy",
            "ecr:DescribeRepositories",
            "ecr:ListImages",
            "ecr:DescribeImages",
            "ecr:BatchGetImage",
            "ecr:InitiateLayerUpload",
            "ecr:UploadLayerPart",
            "ecr:CompleteLayerUpload",
            "ecr:PutImage"
        ],
        "Resource": "arn:aws:ecr:eu-
central-1:123456789012:repository/randserver"
    }]
}
```

To create the policy, execute the following, passing the appropriate path for the JSON document file:

```
$ aws iam create-policy --policy-name EcrPushPullRandserverDevelopers --
policy-document file://./policy.json
    {
        "Policy": {
        "PolicyName": "EcrPushPullRandserverDevelopers",
        "PolicyId": "ANPAITNBFTFWZMI4WFOY6",
        "Arn":
"arn:aws:iam::123456789012:policy/EcrPushPullRandserverDevelopers",
        "Path": "/",
```

```
                "DefaultVersionId": "v1",
                "AttachmentCount": 0,
                "PermissionsBoundaryUsageCount": 0,
                "IsAttachable": true,
                "CreateDate": "2018-10-25T12:00:15Z",
                "UpdateDate": "2018-10-25T12:00:15Z"
                }
        }
```

The final step is then to attach the policy to the group, so that johndoe and all future developers of this application can use the repository from their workstation, just like we did previously:

```
$ aws iam attach-group-policy --group-name randserver-developers --policy-
arn arn:aws:iam::123456789012:policy/EcrPushPullRandserverDevelopers
```

Use images stored on ECR in Kubernetes

You may recall, in Chapter 7, *A Production-Ready Cluster* that we attached the IAM policy, AmazonEC2ContainerRegistryReadOnly, to the instance profile used by our cluster nodes. This allows our nodes to fetch any images in any repository in the AWS account where the cluster resides.

In order to use an ECR repository in this manner, you should set the image field of the pod template on your manifest to point to it, such as in the following example:

```
image: 123456789012.dkr.ecr.eu-central-1.amazonaws.com/randserver:0.0.1.
```

Tagging images

Whenever a Docker image is pushed to a registry, we need to identify the image with a tag. A tag can be any alphanumeric string: latest stable v1.7.3 and even c31b1656da70a0b0b683b060187b889c4fd1d958 are both perfectly valid examples of tags that you might use to identify an image that you push to ECR.

Depending on how your software is developed and versioned, what you put in this tag might be different. There are three main strategies that might be adopted depending on different types of applications and development processes that that we might need to generate images for.

Version Control System (VCS) references

When you build images from software where the source is managed in a version control system, such as Git, the simplest way of tagging your images in this case is to utilize the commit ID (often referred to as a SHA when using Git) from your VCS. This gives you a very simple way to check exactly which version of your code is currently running at any one time.

This first strategy is often adopted for applications where small changes are delivered in an incremental fashion. New versions of your images might be pushed multiple times a day and automatically deployed to testing and production-like environments. Good examples of these kinds of applications that are web applications and other software delivered as a service.

By pushing a commit ID through an automated testing and release pipeline, you can easily generate deployment manifests for an exact revision of your software.

Semantic versions

However, this strategy becomes more cumbersome and harder to deal with if you are building container images that are intended to be used by many users, whether that be multiple users within your organisation or even when you publish images publicly for third parties to use. With applications like these, it can be helpful to use a semantic version number that has some meaning, helping those that depend on you image decide if it safe to move to a newer version.

A common scheme for these sorts of images is called **Semantic Versioning (SemVer)**. This is a version number made up of three individual numbers separated by dots. These numbers are known as the **MAJOR**, **MINOR**, and **PATCH** version. A semantic version number lays out these numbers in the form `MAJOR.MINOR.PATCH`. When a number is incremented, the less significant numbers to the right are reset to `0`.

These version numbers give downstream users useful information about how a new version might affect compatibility:

- The `PATCH` version is incremented whenever a bug or security fix is implemented that maintains backwards compatibility
- The `MINOR` version is incremented whenever a new feature is added that maintains backwards compatibility
- Any changes that break backwards compatibility should increment the `MAJOR` version number

This is useful because users of your images know that MINOR or PATCH level changes are unlikely to break anything, so only basic testing should be required when upgrading to a new version. But if upgrading to a new MAJOR version, they ought to check and test the impact on the changes, which might require changes to configuration or integration code.

 You can read more about SemVer at https://semver.org/.

Upstream version numbers

Often, when we when build container images that repackage existing software, it is desirable to use the original version number of the packaged software itself. Sometimes, it can help to add a suffix to version the configuration that you're using to package that software with.

In larger organisations, it can be common to package software tools with configuration files with organisation-specific default settings. You might find it useful to version the configuration files as well as the software tool.

If I were packaging the MySQL database for use in my organisation, an image tag might look like 8.0.12-c15, where 8.0.12 refers to the upstream MySQL version and c15 is a version number I have created for the MySQL configuration files included in my container image.

Labelling images

If you have an even moderately complex workflow for developing and releasing your software, you might quickly find yourself wanting to add even more semantic information about your images into its tag than just a simple version number. This can quickly become unwieldy, as you will need to modify your build and deployment tooling whenever you want to add some extra information.

Thankfully, Docker images carry around labels that can be used to store whatever metadata is relevant to your image.

Adding a label to your image is done at build time, using the LABEL instruction in your Dockerfile. The LABEL instruction accepts multiple key value pairs in this format:

```
LABEL <key>=<value> <key>=<value> ...
```

Using this instruction, we can store any arbitrary metadata that we find useful on our images. And because the metadata is stored inside the image, unlike tags, it can't be changed. By using appropriate image labels, we can discover the exact revision from our VCS, even if an image has been given an opaque tag, such as latest or stable.

If you want to set these labels dynamically at build time, you can also make use of the ARG instruction in your Dockerfile.

Let's look at an example of using build arg's to set labels. Here is an example Dockerfile:

```
FROM scratch
ARG SHA
ARG BEAR=Paddington
LABEL git-commit=$GIT_COMMIT \
      favorite-bear=$BEAR \
      marmalade="5 jars"
```

When we build the container, we can pass values for our labels using the --build-arg flag. This is useful when we want to pass dynamic values such as a Git commit reference:

```
docker build --build-arg SHA=`git rev-parse --short HEAD` -t bear .
```

As with the labels that Kubernetes allows you to attach to the objects in your cluster, you are free to label your images with whatever scheme you choose, and save whatever metadata makes sense for your organisation.

The **Open Container Initiative** (**OCI**), an organization that promotes standards for container runtimes and their image formats, has proposed a standard set of labels that can be used to provide useful metadata that can then be used by other tools that understand them. If you decide to add labels to your container images, choosing to use part or all of this set of labels might be a good place to start.

These labels are all prefixed with `org.opencontainers.image` so that they don't collide with any ad hoc labels that you may already be using:

- * `org.opencontainers.image.title`: This should be a human-readable title for the image. For example, `Redis`.
- `org.opencontainers.image.description`: This should be a human - readable description of the image. For example, `Redis is an open source key-value store`.
- `org.opencontainers.image.created`: This should contain the date and time that the image was created. It should be formatted as per RFC 3339. For example, `2018-11-25T22:14:00Z`.
- `org.opencontainers.image.authors`: This should contain contact information about the people or organisations responsible for this image. Typically, this might be an email address, or other relevant contact information. For example, `Edward Robinson <ed@errm.co.uk>`.
- `org.opencontainers.image.url`: This should be a URL where more information about the image can be found. For example, `https://github.com/errm/kubegratulations`.
- `org.opencontainers.image.documentation`: This should be a URL where documentation about the image can be found. For example, `https://github.com/errm/kubegratulations/wiki`.
- `org.opencontainers.image.source`: This should be a URL where the source code used to build an image can be found. You might use it to link to a project page on a version control repository, such as GitHub, GitLab, or Bitbucket. For example, `https://github.com/errm/kubegratulations`.
- `org.opencontainers.image.version`: This could be a semantic version for the software packaged in this image, or it could be a label or tag used in your VCS. For example, `1.4.7`.
- `org.opencontainers.image.revision`: This should be a reference to a revision in your VCS, such as a Git commit SHA. For example, `e2f3bbdf80acd3c96a68ace41a4ac699c203a6a4`.
- `org.opencontainers.image.vendor`: This should be the name of an organisation or individual distributing the image. For example, **Apache Software Foundation (ASF)**.
- `org.opencontainers.image.licenses`: If your image contains software covered by a specific licence, you can list them here. You should use SPDX identifiers to refer to the licences. You can find the full list at `https://spdx.org/licenses/`. For example, `Apache-2.0`.

Summary

In this chapter, we've learned how easy it is to provision a Docker registry to store images for our applications on AWS in a reproducible and foolproof fashion using ECR.

We discovered how to push images from our own workstations, how to use IAM permissions to restrict access to our images, and how to allow Kubernetes to pull container images directly from ECR.

You should now be aware of several strategies for tagging your images and know how to add additional labels to your images to store metadata about their contents, and you have learned about the standard labels recommended by the Open Container Initiative image specification.

Other Books You May Enjoy

If you enjoyed this book, you may be interested in these other books by Packt:

Effective DevOps with AWS - Second Edition
Yogesh Raheja, Giuseppe Borgese, Nathaniel Felsen

ISBN: 978-1-78953-997-4

- Implement automatic AWS instance provisioning using CloudFormation
- Deploy your application on a provisioned infrastructure with Ansible
- Manage infrastructure using Terraform
- Build and deploy a CI/CD pipeline with Automated Testing on AWS
- Understand the container journey for a CI/CD pipeline using AWS ECS
- Monitor and secure your AWS environment

Practical DevOps - Second Edition
Joakim Verona

ISBN: 978-1-78839-257-0

- Understand how all deployment systems fit together to form a larger system
- Set up and familiarize yourself with all the tools you need to be efficient with DevOps
- Design an application suitable for continuous deployment systems with DevOps in mind
- Store and manage your code effectively using Git, Gerrit, Gitlab, and more
- Configure a job to build a sample CRUD application
- Test your code using automated regression testing with Jenkins Selenium
- Deploy your code using tools such as Puppet, Ansible, Palletops, Chef, and Vagrant

Leave a review - let other readers know what you think

Please share your thoughts on this book with others by leaving a review on the site that you bought it from. If you purchased the book from Amazon, please leave us an honest review on this book's Amazon page. This is vital so that other potential readers can see and use your unbiased opinion to make purchasing decisions, we can understand what our customers think about our products, and our authors can see your feedback on the title that they have worked with Packt to create. It will only take a few minutes of your time, but is valuable to other potential customers, our authors, and Packt. Thank you!

Index

Made in the USA
Middletown, DE
16 August 2019